THE LIBRARY OF TRADITIONAL WISDOM

The Library of Traditional Wisdom has as its aim to present a series of works founded on Tradition, this term being defined as the transmission, over time, of permanent and universal truths, whose written sources are the revealed Scriptures as well as the writings of the great spiritual masters.

This series is thus dedicated to the *Sophia Perennis* or *Religio Perennis* which is the timeless metaphysical truth underlying the diverse religions, together with its essential methodological consequences.

It is in the light of the *Sophia Perennis*, which views every religion "from within," that may be found the keys for an adequate understanding which, joined to the sense of the sacred, alone can safeguard the irreplaceable values and genuine spiritual possibilities of the great religions.

The Transcendent Unity of Religions, *Faber and Faber, 1953*

Spiritual Perspectives and Human Facts, *Faber and Faber, 1954*

Language of the Self, *Ganesh, Madras, 1959*

Gnosis: Divine Wisdom, *John Murray, 1959*

Stations of Wisdom, *John Murray, 1961*

Understanding Islam, *Allen and Unwin, 1963*

Light on the Ancient Worlds, *Perennial Books, 1966*

In the Tracks of Buddhism, *Allen and Unwin, 1968*

Dimensions of Islam, *Allen and Unwin, 1969*

Logic and Transcendence, *Harper and Row, 1975*

The Transcendent Unity of Religions, *Revised Edition, Harper and Row, 1975*

Islam and the Perennial Philosophy, *World of Islam Festival Publishing Company, 1976*

Esoterism as Principle and as Way, *Perennial Books, 1981*

Castes and Races, *Perennial Books, 1981*

IN PREPARATION:

From the Divine to the Human, *World Wisdom Books*

Christianity/Islam, *World Wisdom Books*

SUFISM
Veil and Quintessence

FRITHJOF SCHUON

Translated by William Stoddart

WORLD WISDOM BOOKS

First published as
Sufism: Voile et Quintessence ©1979 Dervy Livres

Sufism: Veil and Quintessence
Copyright ©1981 by World Wisdom Books

For information address World Wisdom Books,
4211 E. Third St., Bloomington, Indiara 47401.

Designed by Marc Cheshire
The cover motif is an Islamic geometric
symbol of the Divine Unity.

Library of Congress 81-69573
ISBN 0-941532-00-3

Table of Contents

Preface

"Veil" *(hijāb)* and "quintessence" *(lubāb)*: two words which are opposite in meaning, both as symbols and as doctrinal expressions, and which refer respectively to the outward and the inward, or to contingency and necessity. When we discern in Sufism a "veil," this must here be understood, not in the completely general sense that applies to every expression of the transcendent, but in a particular sense that pertains to historical Sufism by reason of its being bound up with a denominational psychology and an ardent temperament. Nor, in this case, is the term "esoterism" entirely clear-cut; it has to be interpreted at various degrees or from different points of view. To enable us to give an uninhibited account of quintessential Sufism, it is necessary to speak first of all of certain veilings which all too often prevent one from approaching it serenely and from perceiving its true nature.

When one speaks of doctrinal "quintessence," this may mean one of two things: firstly, the loftiest and subtlest part of a doctrine, and it is in this sense that Sufis distinguish between the "husk" *(qishr)* and the "marrow" *(lubb)*; and secondly, an integral doctrine envisaged in respect of its fundamental and necessary nature, and thus leaving aside all outward trappings and all superstructure. To give an account of Sufism, one could in fact restrict oneself, either to dealing with the mystery of the "unicity of the Real" *(wahdat al-Wujūd)*, or to providing a survey of the characteristic and therefore indispensable elements of

1

the doctrine as a whole; it goes without saying, that the two points of view are bound up with each other in principle, for to seek out the essential in itself and hence in simplicity prompts one to look for it also in complexity, and conversely. The present book does not separate these two intentions.

Some have thought to serve the reputation of Sufism, or to safeguard its mystery, by declaring that it is not a system as are philosophies, but that on the contrary it presents itself as a collection of formulations and symbolisms that have freely sprung forth from the intellect and from inspiration. Leaving aside the fact that the one does not preclude the other, we do not see how there could possibly be anything pejorative in the notion of a system: every cosmos, from the stars to the smallest crystal, is a system in the sense that each one reflects the homogeneity of the principial order; the universe is woven of necessity and liberty, of mathematical rigor and musical play, of geometry and poetry. It would do an injustice to Sufism to assert that it is in no wise capable of systematic formulation, or that it is not, like every other integral doctrine, a crystal that captures the divine Light, and refracts it in terms of a language that is both particular and universal.

All the same, doctrinal expressions are not meant to be exhaustive, their function being simply to act as landmarks for a complex truth and with a view to the Inexpressible. This is what modern critics fail to understand when they reproach the ancient doctrines for being both dogmatic and insufficient. In reality a theoretical expression can only be an "allusive indication" *(ishārah)* whose implications are limitless; and they are limitless to the very degree that the thesis is fundamental. For it is not a question of inventing truth, it is a question of remembering it.

Objectivity is the essence of intelligence, but intelligence is often far from being in conformity with its essence. In reality, objectivity may be seen as the quasi-moral quality—or condition—of intelligence; the latter becomes mere cleverness or ingenuity as soon as it is separated from the former. Ingenuity may be interested, it may serve some thesis or other; but objectivity, by definition, cannot involve itself arbitrarily; moreover it has no need to do so, since no secondary paradox can impair the essential truth with which it deals. Man may have his attachments, his instinct of self-preservation may lead him into error; and this is why, in many instances, to be objective is to die a little; "there is no right higher than that of truth." The present book contains criticisms which at first sight are not at all in the interest of its fundamental thesis, but this thesis has nothing to fear from secondary observations that seem to detract from it, given that a spirituality cannot be substantially at the mercy of human imperfections. "If thou wouldst reach the kernel," said Eckhart, "thou must break the shell."

There is a "contingent" Islam just as there is an "absolute" Islam. In order to separate the second from certain debatable elements pertaining only to the human clothing of the Message and not to the Message in itself, we are obliged also to give an account of the first, especially since esoterism is at stake, but it is obviously "absolute" Islam that matters to us, and it is of this that we shall speak starting from the chapter on quintessential esoterism. The distinction between a dimension that is "absolute" and one that is "relative" is obviously valid for every religion, but it is only Islam that we intend to deal with in this book. In any event, only pure Revelation can be the vehicle of esoterism *de jure*: "by right," and not only "in fact."

*

*　*

The intrinsic orthodoxy of Islam results from its Message: God *(Allāh)*, the Prophet *(Muhammad)*, Prayer *(Salāt)*, Almsgiving *(Zakāt)*, the Fast *(Siyām)*, the Pilgrimage *(Hajj)*; to which the Holy War *(Jihād)* may be added on occasion.

3

God: the Absolute, is real; that is to say, He is Reality *(Haqq)*, Necessary Being *(al-Wujūd al-Mutlaq)*, therefore That which cannot not be, whereas things can either be or not be; being unique, He excludes all that is not He; being total, He includes all that is possible or existent; there is nothing "alongside" Him and nothing "outside" Him. — The Prophet: this thesis states the very principle of Revelation, its modes and its rhythms; if there is a God and if there are men, there must necessarily also be Messengers of God. — Prayer: likewise, if there is a God and if there are men, there is necessarily a dialogue; it is given by this very confrontation. — Almsgiving: this principle results from the fact that man in not alone, that he lives in society and that he must know, and feel, that "the other" is also "I"; whence the necessity for charity at all levels. — The Fast: this principle is founded on the necessity for sacrifice; whoever receives must also give, and further, the body is not everything, any more than is the world; the spirit can ennoble matter but matter is nonetheless fallen. — The Pilgrimage: this is the principle of the return to the source, to the primordial sanctuary, and thus also to the heart. — Holy War: this results from the right, and in certain cases the duty, to defend the Truth; esoterically or even morally, it becomes the struggle against passional and mental darkness; one must overcome the inborn worship of the world and the ego so as to be integrated into the reign of Peace *(dār as-Salām)*.

All these principles, which confer on Islam its incontestable character and its universality are also to be found in ourselves; their outward manifestations derive all their meaning — metaphysically and contemplatively speaking — from their archetypes which are both transcendent and immanent.

CHAPTER 1

Ellipsis and Hyperbolism in Arab Rhetoric

The Arab style favors synthetic and indirect figures of speech: ellipsis, synecdoche and metonymy are common, as are also metaphor, hyperbole and tautology. The Semite has a propensity always to distinguish between an "essence" and a "form" and does not hesitate to sacrifice the homogeneity of the latter to the veracity of the former, so that in Semitic texts of a religious or poetic nature one must always perceive the intention behind the expression, and not overlook it because of some formal incoherence; and it is not only the spiritual intention that must be discovered, but also the emotion which determines its outpouring and its verbal concretization. Thus hyperbole often conveys an emotion provoked by a direct perception of the spiritual reality to be defined; but what counts above all is the use of hyperbole to indicate a precise, but implicit, relationship, which confers on the proposition all its meaning, and by this very fact compensates or abolishes any appearance of absurdity in its wording.

It is true that Arab stylists demand both logical clarity and dialectic efficacy in accordance, respectively, with their sense of formal correctness *(fasāhah)* and of rhetoric *(balāghah)* bent on soundness of content. But this in no wise conflicts with the Semitic tendency towards indirect expression, since for the Arabs a thing is clear if in their opinion it is well said; the frequent use of "disguise" *(kinā-yah)* shows on the contrary that for the Arab it is natural to "embellish" an expression by making it less direct and, from his point of view, all the more rich. Nevertheless in the Arab style there are as it were two poles: one fully corresponding to what we have just described, and the other of a more abstract or logician-like character; these two poles are crystallized respectively in the schools of Kufa and Basra, the first being based on scriptural paradigms and thus possessing an illustrative and empirical character, and the second inspired by a more principial or theoretical conception of language; this second form of rhetoric predominates in theological, scientific and philosophical writings including the strictly doctrinal treatises of the Sufis.

But what concerns us here is the Arabic language in its most spontaneous expression, with its metaphorical and readily hyperbolic style, a style which takes its inspiration from the Sunna and, consciously or not, from the ancient poetry. Since one cannot help taking into account the ethnic or psychological conditioning of a language, apart from its strictly spiritual foundation, we must not pass over in silence here the noble impulsiveness, and the veneer of rashness resulting therefrom, characteristic of the ancient Arabs, who would draw the sword "for a yea or a nay"; this is true to the point that the Koran had to state specifically that God did not hold believers responsible for their unconsidered oaths. At the level of language, the vice of an impulsive hyperbolism — especially in a spiritual context — would be seriously disconcerting if allowance were not made for an explosive temperament, noble in its very sincerity.

We have mentioned above the often indirect character of Arab rhetoric, and it would be fitting to dwell on this a little longer. The Gospel injunction not to cast pearls before swine nor to give what is sacred to dogs, apart from its obvious and universal significance, indicates at the same time — and as if by accident — a specifically Semitic trait: direct and naked truth is both too precious and too dangerous, it intoxicates and it kills, and it runs the risk of

6

being profaned and of inciting revolts; it is like wine which must be sealed, and which Islam prohibits, or like woman who must be covered, and whom in fact Islam veils. The spiritual style of the Semites is often full of reticences and indirect figures of speech; it is like a subtle play of veilings and unveilings; the inspired word is an inviolable bride, and the aspirant must be worthy of her even at the level of mere language.[1] Esoteric precaution has thus impregnated all Arab rhetoric, and has determined a kind of modesty or discretion on the plane of verbal manifestation, as well as a particular aesthetic: that is to say there is also present an element of play or art, of musical calligraphy, if one prefer. Language appears to the Arab almost as an end in itself, as an autonomous substance which pre-exists in relation to its contents; like Universal Existence, which is its prototype, language encloses us ontologically in the truth, whether we wish it or not: before all words, its all-embracing meaning is "Be" *(Kun)*; it is Divine in its essence. "In the beginning was the Word."

Veiling and overflowing are as it were the two complementary poles of the Arab mentality in particular and of the Moslem mentality in general. The Moslem spirit is rooted in the certainty of the Absolute and oriented towards this certainty and its object; but this awareness of the highest and most intransigent Truth has as its human complement an emotivity all the more fulgurating; and this emotivity is compensated by a profound generosity; here we have in mind not so much the Bedouin temperament in itself as its enhancement through Islam; which is to say that the two opposite and complementary charac-

1. This mentality, or this principle, evokes the initiatic symbolism of Perseus and Andromeda, and thus also of the victory over Medusa. The symbolism of the truth-bride is also found in the Song of Songs, and again, from an iconographic point of view, in the Black Virgins: "I am black but beautiful" likewise says the Shulamite. Blackness represents the secret and supra-formal character of gnosis, although in certain cases — as applied to Jerusalem for example — it may have the negative meaning of distress.

7

teristics just mentioned pertain to the genius of Islam as well as — and even more profoundly — to the positive mentality of the Arab race. This ternary, "Truth-Victory-Generosity," describes the very soul of the Prophet, in which the genius of Islam and that of the Arab race are fused: consciousness of the Absolute has as its dynamic repercussion the holy war, for the Absolute excludes all that is not it, being in this respect like a devouring fire; but at the same time the Absolute is the Infinite, which is maternal and which encompasses all, and in this respect consciousness of the One will engender appeasing and charitable attitudes, such as almsgiving and forgiveness.

*

* *

Arab hyperbole, as indicated above, has the function of indirectly throwing into relief a particular relationship, one which is not expressed but which must be perceived by means of the apparent absurdity of the image. For example, a *hadīth*[2] relates that a woman entered Paradise in advance of the elect for the simple reason that she had brought up her children well; this means that the fact of having brought up her children with perfect abnegation and with the best possible result manifests the sanctity of the mother. As for being in advance of the elect — on the face of it a contradictory idea — this is simply a metaphor; spatial "advancement" here represents an advantage of easiness, not of distance or of movement; which is to say that there are simple souls who enter Paradise relatively easily, or in other words, without having to undergo the great trials of the heroes of spirituality. Needless to say the *hadīth* makes no allusion to the degrees of Paradise; it has no other intention than to emphasize the facility accorded to humble but constant merits, which presupposes moreover a totally religious ambience. Its teaching is as follows: the believer who performs his necessary duties to

2. A saying of the Prophet. Plural: *ahādīth.*

8

perfection, without concerning himself with anything else except religion and this duty, however humble it may be, will go to Paradise if he perseveres to the end; but this is no recipe of easiness, for each has his own nature, vocation, duty and destiny.[3]

In an analogous manner, the Prophet said that "those who receive the severest punishment on the Day of Resurrection will be those who imitate what God has created," or "who make representations of (living) things," and that God will then order them to give life to the images, which they will be incapable of doing. When the Prophet expresses himself thus the fact of fashioning images implies the intention of equalling the Creator, and thus of denying His uniqueness and transcendence; if the punishment is the severest possible — which in this case seems exaggerated and even absurd — this is because the plastic arts are identified in the psychology of the nomadic and monotheistic Semites with a kind of luciferianism or idolatry, and thus with the greatest of sins, or with sin as such.

When some *ahādīth* speak of a woman who was damned because she allowed her cat to die of hunger, or of a prostitute who was saved because she gave a drink of water to a dog, the meaning is that man is saved or damned by virtue of his essence, even if it is veiled by characteristics opposed to it, but which are nevertheless peripheral and consequently accidental. Here the act is not the efficient cause, but the sign of a fundamental cause which resides in the very nature of the individual; the act is the manifested criterion of a fundamental and decisive quality, so much so that there is no reason to be surprised by the fact that an apparently trifling act should have an effect which is quasi-absolute or incommensurate with its cause.

An example of hyperbolism at once veiling and unveiling a hidden relationship — a relationship outside of

3. This is one of the meanings of the verse which appears several times in the Koran: "No soul shall bear the burden of another."

which the enunciation remains unintelligible—such an example is provided by this saying of Junayd: "A moment of forgetfulness of the Lord ruins a thousand years of service (to God)." Here again, the forgetfulness of God is identified with sin as such; and it is precisely the almost insane exaggeration of the image which proves it. Here virtue or merit—the only virtue or the only merit—is the remembrance of God; Junayd wishes to underline that this remembrance is the quintessence of every virtue and by this fact constitutes the whole reason for the existence of the human state. The same remark can be applied to this other saying of the same saint: "A thousand years of obedience cannot annul a moment of disobedience towards God,"[4] with the sole difference that here it is obedience that is identified with virtue as such; and the same remark applies equally *mutatis mutandis*, to the following passage from Samarqandi: "Even if a man has performed the prayer of the inhabitants of Heaven and earth . . . If I *(Allāh)* were to find that in his heart there still remains an atom of love for the world, be this a desire to please the eyes or ears of someone else, or a worldly ambition . . . I would extirpate his love for Me from his heart . . . until he forgot Me . . . "[5] Here again, the exaggeration serves to indicate a particular relationship which gives the whole meaning to the saying, namely, that hypocrisy, like the Christian notion of pride, sums up every possible vice of the spirit; being the very quality of evil, no quantity of

4. "I am a slave and have no liberty; I shall go wherever God will order me to go, be it to Paradise or to hell." This saying of Junayd shows that he looks on obedience as the most perfect conformity to the Will—or the Nature—of God, or that he envisages perfection under the aspect of obedience; but here again, a spiritual sublimity entails a logical or rhetorical defect for, apart from the fact that the Koran does not ordain that any believer should go to hell, a pious man who thinks like Junayd obviously cannot be damned, since he is obedient to God.

5. Quite apart from the literal meaning, one might wonder whether it is permissible, or opportune, to express oneself as if God were speaking . . .

good can annul it.[6] It is true that its opposite, sincerity, the fundamental quality of goodness, can similarly conquer every quantitative evil; but the presence of sincerity excludes hypocrisy, precisely, thus this remedy is not accessible to the hypocrite. Taken literally, all these sayings are contrary to Koranic doctrine according to which Divine punishment is in proportion to human transgression while Divine reward immensely surpasses our merit; the legitimacy—in any case quite relative—of these sayings consequently resides in their intention alone, namely, in the stress that they put on the "sin against the Holy Ghost," whatever be the angle of vision; this stress is clearly their whole excuse and reason for existence, but cannot be a total justification.

In view of the spirituality of a Junayd and a Samarqandi, we may perhaps deduce from their verbal excesses what was their "station" *(maqām)*: a reduction of all temporal awareness to an instant of eternity made of pure adequation to the Real, and thus free from all "association" (of other realities to God: *shirk*), from every "covering up" (or "stifling" of the Truth: *kufr*), from every hypocrisy *(nifāq)*; this is practically the meaning of the expression "son of the present moment" *(ibn al-waqt)* which is applied to the Sufis.

Be that as it may, if the sayings quoted—and other sayings of the same kind—can be justified by their intentions, or rather can justify their authors, they remain subject to caution in other respects, first of all in respect of intelligibility—a spiritual saying has the right to be unintelligible on condition that it is not absurd—and then in re-

6. Let us note that the reference to the "heart" indicates that what is in question is the essence of the individual, although the idea "atom" weakens this meaning; here there are two "absolutizations" which contradict each other in the flood of the spiritual emotion, which in short mixes together two different propositions. What is only an "atom" cannot be situated in the heart, and what is situated in our essence cannot be reduced to an infinitesimal quantity, morally or spiritually speaking.

11

spect of the esoteric perspective, which cannot coincide purely and simply with an ascetico-mystical perspective. We shall return to this question, which is of capital importance, in the next chapter.[7]

*

* *

The effort to depict the aspects of plenitude and limitlessness of Paradise has given rise to quantitative metaphors which can be accepted without question only if one is either naïve, or on the contrary particularly perspicacious, or else simply resigned to the feebleness of human understanding and of earthly language. The first key to this symbolism is that in it quantity assumes a qualitative role, and that the very excessiveness of the image invites us to go to the root of things; but side by side with the quantitative images, one also finds other hyperboles whose intention may be divined by examining the nature of things. For example: according to tradition, the houris wear seventy dresses, but at the same time these are transparent and one can see the marrow flowing in their bones, "like liquid and luminous honey," we are told; the dresses symbolize the beauties of veiling, and thus of the formal or "liturgical" aspects of beauty, while the marrow represents the uncreated essence, which is none other than an aspect of the Divine Substance, or a kind of emanation from a beatific Divine Quality. That is to say that God makes Himself perceptible through all that is in Paradise; but the connection between the relativity of the created and the absoluteness of the Essence requires an indefinite play of veiling and unveiling, of formal coagulation and compensatory transparence.

7. One will no doubt encounter in the present book inevitable repetitions and perhaps also apparent contradictions, the latter being due to our two-fold obligation to criticize and to justify, in a domain in which the line of demarcation between the permissible and the abusive is unclear.

When one reads that in Paradise the least of the blessed enjoys such and such marvels or delights, that he has so many wives, servants, and so on, one may wonder what those who would appreciate or bear such an oppressive luxury are doing in Paradise; now Islam, as a matter of principle, always includes at its base the most earthly of possibilities—this is a "card in its hand" that it never neglects—and thus places itself at the standpoint, not of grossness but of mercy, at the risk of appearing "earthy" or trivial. Islam demands *a priori* neither detachment from the world nor refinement of taste, but only faith in God and the putting into practice of the Divine Laws, a practice which always implies the fundamental virtues; and it is faith and practice which will transmute the soul of the believer, detach him from the world and refine his tastes. On the one hand, Islam means to capture the most naïve and unpolished of mentalities; but on the other hand it also takes account—in the *aḥādīth*—of the most diverse mentalities, so much so that there are sayings which are addressed to a given character and not to another.

What we have said of the paradisal hyperbolisms applies equally, but in an inverse sense, to infernal imagery: the historical experience of both East and West superabundantly proves that a great deal is necessary to dissuade the sinner from sinning; it is true that the most terrible descriptions of hell may remain ineffective for the most hardened criminals, but when they are effective they too are a part of mercy, since they prevent some souls from becoming lost. But in the eschatological metaphors it is not a question solely of baits and bugbears: the delights and torments are respectively the cosmic equivalents of virtues and vices, merits and demerits, and disclose their true nature in the light of Divine measures. This consideration, it is true, removes us somewhat from questions of rhetoric, but it is necessary here, and it also seems useful to us, at this point, to make the following remark: paradisal or infernal images are always symbolist

13

paraphrases of realities indescribable in sensory terms, whence their excessive character; it would thus be idle to complain from this sole point of view about all that is humanly unimaginable, or unintelligible, even absurd, in the images of Paradise, for example. The fact that earthly man, enclosed in the prison of his five senses, cannot imagine anything other than what they offer him in no wise means that he would not be infinitely happier outside this happy prison, and within vaster and more profound perceptions.

Moreover, to speak as if Paradise adapted itself to every humor of the believer is a way of saying that the believer adapts himself perfectly to the possibilities of Paradise; to use excessive language is thus to say, in earthly terms, that the blessed possess, not five senses only, but innumerable senses opening onto Felicity, analogically and metaphorically speaking; it means at the same time that the blessed are by nature profoundly satisfied with all that the paradisal state offers them. When the Prophet promises a Bedouin who loves horses a winged horse in Paradise, that means, not that the paradisal possibilities will fulfill every possible desire, but that they will realize every possibility of happiness of the believing man; this epithet "believing" is essential, for true faith excludes precisely—and *a fortiori* before God—that man desire just anything. Without faith, no Paradise; with faith, no senseless or harmful desires; and let us recall that every pleasure we can describe as "normal" is a kind of reverberation and consequently an anticipation—no doubt, quite imperfect—of a celestial joy, as the Koran declares: "Each time they are offered a fruit (of Paradise) they will say: 'This is what was offered us before (on earth)': for it is something similar which will be given them . . . " (*Sura of the Cow,* 25). Finally, this should be taken into consideration: the Oriental starts from the idea that in this world below man is easily deprived of what he desires and separated from what he loves; to conclude from this that in

14

Paradise we obtain at once whatever we desire is but a short step, and this step has in fact been crossed with an impeccable and somewhat expeditious logic;[8] the minimization by the Sufis of what might seem like a "celestial nightmare" is the result of this two-edged logic, all the more so in that the Koran itself teaches that the "Divine contentment" *(Ridwān)* granted to the believer is "greater" than the "Garden."

*

* *

Before going any further, let us return for a moment to the question of emotivity or impulsiveness, which is inseparable from the psychological aspect of the use of hyperbole. When reading traditional writings — not forgetting profane literature such as the "Thousand and One Nights" and poetry — one is struck by the facility with which ancient Orientals wept, tore their garments, uttered a great cry, fell down in a swoon if not dead — all this while under the sway of some visual, auditive or mental emotion; this temperament obliges us to recognize the opportuneness of an exoteric religion in some respects pedantic and formalistic, but well fitted to put a brake on thoughtless exuberances.

Metaphorically speaking, the Bedouin is a man who, with a great blow, kills a fly on his wife's cheek, forgetting that in so doing he is striking his wife; this image, despite its aspect of popular humor has the advantage of illustrating straightforwardly the temperament in question. Example: according to some holy man, it is better to be seated in a miserable spot on earth remembering God, than to be seated under a tree in Paradise without remembering Him; the intention of this saying is impeccable and

8. On the basis of the Koranic promise that the blessed "will have whatever they want"; this leaves open the question as to what desires are still possible in Paradise, and also what is the nature of the blessed themselves.

transparent, but the literal sense nevertheless does violence to the Koranic idea of Paradise and the elect. A further example: Ghazālī, in his book on marriage, mentions a bachelor who, dying of the plague, asks for a wife "in order to appear before God according to the Sunna, that is, married"; the absurd serves here to create the sublime.

It it is true that such and such a religion creates or predisposes to such and such sentimental tendencies, it is even more true that Revelation must take account of pre-existing tendencies of this kind and must more or less come to meet them: to offer to souls images at their own level and to transmute these souls without their being aware of it is the very definition of *upāya*, the "provisional means" or the "saving mirage" of Buddhism. The Bedouin is so made that in his heart of hearts he wants to be chief, governor, or king; he is violent, generous and insatiable, his imagination opens not only onto riches and pleasures, but also onto power and glory;[9] it is thus necessary to present him with a Paradise that can captivate him.

Be that as it may, it is quite obvious that pious exaggeration, even pious absurdity, is not the exclusive property of any race nor of any religion: it is encountered notably—always as an inevitable excess or "lesser evil"—in the Christian ambience as well, for example when a devout man, through "humility" or "charity," accuses himself of sins he has not committed, or accuses himself of being the greatest sinner or the vilest of men, or when he acts foolishly in order to be despised, without concerning himself with the effects of his attitudes on the souls of others, and so on.

From another point of view, one must beware of seeing in a certain kind of modern rationality a total superi-

---

9. It is noteworthy how frequently in Arab texts one finds allusions which recall a society at once patriarchal, chivalrous and mercantile: the notions of "ransom" and "redemption," of "debt," "hostage" and "intercession," and others of the kind, seem to be landmarks of Arab psychology.

ority. Contemporary man, in spite of his being marked by certain experiences due to the senescence of humanity, is spiritually soft and ineffective and intellectually ready to commit every possible betrayal, which will seem to him as summits of intelligence, whereas in reality these betrayals are far more absurd than the excesses of simplicity and emotivity of ancient man. In a general way, the man of the "last days" is a blunted creature, and the best proof of this is that the only "dynamism" of which he is still capable is that which tends downwards, and which is no more than a passivity taking advantage of cosmic gravity; it is the agitation of a man who lets himself be carried away by a torrent and who imagines that he is creating this torrent himself by his agitation.

*

*   *

A few words on Arab tautology are called for here, since we have spoken of hyperbole and disparity. As a first example we shall quote the following Koranic passage: "Shall I take other gods apart from Him? If the All-Merciful should wish me harm, their intercession would avail me naught. Truly I should then be in manifest error" (*Sura Yā Sīn*, 23 and 24). The last sentence serves, not to explain what is already obvious, namely that one must not admit false gods, but to underline that this error is, not subtle or occult, hence possibly benefitting from extenuating circumstances, but that it is on the contrary unpardonable, since the truth of the One God imposes itself — as St. Thomas would say — by the superabundance of its clarity; here it is in fact a question of the metaphysical evidence of the Absolute, evidence which subjectively is innate and pre-rational, and objectively is recognizable in the profound nature of things.[10]

10. In our time there is much talk of "sincere" atheism; however, apart from the fact that sincerity neither prevents error from being error nor adds any value to it whatsoever, there is always in this system

17

Another example is provided by a nearby Koranic passage (Verse 47 of the same Sura): "And when it is said to them: give in alms a part of what God has provided for you, those who disbelieve will say to those who are believers: shall we feed someone whom God would feed, if He so willed? You are in manifest error." Here again the final proposition emphasizes the evident nature of the idea expressed in what went before: it means that the state of obscuration of unbelievers is such that charity, which nevertheless is in human nature and thus pertains to the primordial norm *(fitrah)*, appears to them as a patent error, which precisely shows the measure of their perversion. Unbelievers cannot reconcile the Divine Omnipotence with human freedom, and in this they are "hypocrites" *(munāfiqūn)* since everyday experience proves that man is free; and what proves it above all is the distinction that every man makes between the state of a creature who is free and that of one who is not, a spontaneous distinction which constitutes the very notion of freedom: the fact that the freedom of creatures is determined by "Divine choice," or that it merely reflects in contingency Divine Freedom or All-Possibility, in no wise invalidates the concrete reality of our free will, without which there could be no question of the moral notions of merit and demerit.

*

* *

Two examples of doctrinal enunciation by means of contradiction are the following Koranic expressions: "He punishes whomsoever He will and He pardons whomsoever He will" (a recurring idea expressed in different ways), and: "I take refuge in the Lord of the dawn, from the evil of that which He has created" (*Sura of the Dawn*, 1-2); the first of these expressions seems to imply that God is arbitrary since He acts apparently without motive, and

of sincerity — or "sincerist" narcissism — a point which constitutes total sin, and which seals off entry to Truth and Mercy.

the second, that He is evil since He causes evil. The key to the correct interpretation is provided by the very definition of God, as it results from the "most beautiful Names" *(Al-Asmā' al-husnā)*, and above all from the Names of Mercy which appear at the head of every Sura. The question which arises is thus the following: how can God punish since "He does what He wishes," and how can He cause or create evil when He is the All-Merciful *(Rahmān, Rahīm)*, the Holy *(Quddūs)*, and the Just *('Adl)*? The answer should be: to assert that God punishes and forgives according to His good pleasure means, not that He is arbitrary, but that this "good pleasure" represents motives which escape our limited understanding;[11] and to say that God creates evil means, not that He wills it as evil, but that He produces it indirectly as a fragment — or as an infinitesimal constitutive element — of a "greater good," whose extent compensates and absorbs that of evil. This truth perhaps requires some further precisions which we shall give here although they go outside the framework of our general subject, and although we have already given them on other occasions and may have to come back to them in the course of the present book: by definition, every evil is a "part" and never a "totality"; and these negations or fragmentary privations, which are the various forms of evil, are inevitable since the world, not being God and unable to be Him, is of necessity situated outside God. But in respect of their cosmic function as necessary elements of a total good, evils are in a certain way integrated into this good, and it is this point of view that makes it possible to affirm that metaphysically there is no evil; the notion of evil presupposes in fact a fragmentary vision of things, characteristic of creatures, who are them-

11. The story of Moses accompanying a mysterious and paradoxical master (Koran, *Sura of the Cave*, 65-82) furnishes the classic example of this problem, at least on the human level; and what is true as regards the master in question is true for all the more reason as regards God.

19

selves fragments; man is a "fragmentary totality."[12]

Evil, as we have seen, is in the world because the world is not God; now from a certain point of view—one of which the Vedantists are especially aware—the world is "none other than God"; *Māyā* is *Ātmā*, *Samsāra* is *Nirvāna*; from this point of view evil does not exist, and this is precisely the point of view of the macrocosmic totality.[13] This is suggested in the Koran by means of the following antinomy: on the one hand it declares that good "comes from God" and that evil "comes from yourselves," and on the other hand it says that "everything comes from God" (*Sura of Women*, 78 and 79), the first idea having to be understood on the basis of the second, which is more universal and therefore more real; it is the difference between fragmentary vision and total truth. The fact that the two verses almost follow one another—the more universal coming first—proves moreover the lack of concern of sacred dialectic with surface contradictions, and the importance that it attaches to penetration and synthesis.[14]

And this brings us back to our more general subject, the question of antinomic expressions in the Koran. An example that has become classical is found in the follow-

12. To solve the rational problem of the incompatibility between the existence of evil and the goodness of God, curiously feeble arguments have sometimes been used: maintaining for example that evil arises, as a simple contrast and in a completely extrinsic manner, from the stipulations of some law—just as a shadow is cast by an object—or that it arises by contrast with our conventional attitudes and so on, as if God would condemn the entire man for such basically unreal transgressions.

13. This is also the legitimate aspect of pantheism; pantheism is illegitimate when it is given an exclusive and unconditional application, valid from every point of view and making things appear as "parts" of God, *quod absit*; the error is in the philosophy, not in the term.

14. Cf. likewise this antinomy: "This is naught but a reminder unto creation, for whomsoever amongst you would follow the straight path. But this ye will not, unless God wills, the Lord of Creation." (*Sura of the Overthrowing*, 27-29).

ing verse: "There is nothing that resembles (God), and He it is who hears, who sees" (*Sura of Counsel*, 11). The flagrant contradiction between the first assertion and the second—which, precisely, establishes a comparison and thereby proves that an analogy between things and God exists—has the function of showing that this obvious analogy, without which no single thing would be possible, in no wise implies an imaginable resemblance and does not abolish in the least the absolute transcendence of the Divine Principle.

*

* *

The Western reader frequently is shocked—and one cannot blame him for this—by the juxtaposition of terms with no obvious connection between them, for example when the Prophet "seeks refuge in God from hunger and treachery"; now in both cases—hunger and treachery—it is a question of earthly insecurity, purely physical in the first instance, social and moral in the second. This way of suggesting something that is precise by means of certain of its aspects—which appear incongruous in the absence of their common denominator—is not exclusively Arab, and is also found in the Bible and in the majority of Sacred Books, perhaps even in all; at all events language contains the possibility of indirect suggestion which runs parallel to the purely descriptive role of the words and gives rise to the most diverse modalities and combinations.

A feature of Islam which particularly disconcerts Westerners is what might be called its "belittling of the human"; this feature is explained by the concern to relate every greatness to God alone[15] and to forestall the emergence of a "humanism," that is, to forestall a way of looking at things which leads to a cult of Titanesque and Luci-

15. As is declared in one of the most celebrated *ahādīth*: "There is no power and no strength but in God."

ferian man. The apparent tautologies in the Koran which seem to belittle the Prophets must be interpreted in the light of this concern: if a given "Messenger" is called "one of the just"[16], this is because no other aspect is of interest in the Islamic perspective. Whatever goes beyond "justice" and "piety" — and which for this reason cannot be an example for simple believers — is on the one hand a mystery with which the common religion does not have to concern itself, and on the other hand a quality whose glory belongs to God alone. A factor that must not be lost sight of is that in the Koran it is God and not man who speaks, and one of the reasons for the existence of certain disconcerting expressions is precisely to recall the smallness of the human, not for its own sake, but in the interest of man, and in connection with the doctrine of Unity.[17]

*

* *

Antinomy is doubtless not of the same order as hyperbole; it is nevertheless related to hyperbolic exaggeration in the sense that, like the latter, it indicates an implicit relationship which gives the surface contradiction all its meaning.[18] In both of these cases, as also in that of tautology, it is a question of a language which is both abrupt

16. The word *sālih*, translated here as "just," comprises the ideas of norm, equilibrium, betterment, appeasement and return to original perfection: this is everything that Islam "officially" requires of "Messengers."

17. The Islamic morality of smallness, obedience and servitude, has little chance of being understood in an age of false liberty and of revolt. Certainly one has every right to rebel against purely human oppressions; but, this contingent question apart, one does not have the choice of wishing for anything other than to resign oneself to the Divine mold, which is Origin, Archetype, Norm and Goal, and alone gives peace of heart, by allowing us to be truly what we are. It is in this acceptance of our absolute destiny that true freedom is realized, but this can only be "in Him" and "through Him," and over and above all our worldly options.

18. It goes without saying that antinomy is not a means of the

22

and indirect, manifesting on the one hand sacred emotion and modesty with regard to precious truths, and on the other the dazzling supra-rationality of the Divine order.

If the logical coherence of the wording of a passage is neither a criterion nor a guarantee of truth or sanctity, neither is the obscure and more or less paradoxical character of a given style of language — within certain limits, at least — a sign of error or weakness; apart from the fact that sacred language may in some respects be a "shock therapy" rather than a neutral communication,[19] it inevitably contains infinitely more than ordinary language, whence a rhetoric of key words which does not necessarily tally with logic pure and simple; and what is true of sacred language properly so-called may also be the case for the spiritual language inspired by it. Certainly logical expression, or the homogeneous and coherent surface of language, may be the vehicle of the highest truth and thus also of sanctity, and it would be absurd to maintain the contrary;[20] but consciousness of the Absolute may equally well fracture, so to speak, the outward form of language, and in this case — but in this case only — it must be admitted that the truth justifies its expression, and moreover it proves it by the perfume of the expression itself. One cannot however assert — and this is a completely different question — that the spiritual worth of a man is always the guarantee of his dialectical means, given the possible tyranny of his surroundings or of conventions, of which he may not be conscious and for which *a fortiori* he is not responsible; unless he make himself their spokesman by affinity or vocation, be this only with a superficial layer of his being.

ordinary dialectic of logicians; moreover, rhetoric and dialectic merge into one another at the level of sacred or sapiential expression.

19. In the formulas of *Zen*, the element "shock" has precedence over the element "information" proper to language, which is possible because shock informs in its turn and in its way.

20. Witness the *Bhagavadgītā*, whose language appears as a perfectly simple and homogeneous surface.

CHAPTER 2

The Exo-Esoteric Symbiosis

To speak of spirituality is *ipso facto* to raise the question of the sources of knowledge, which in this case are revelation, inspiration, intellection, and secondarily also reflection; one must know exactly what is meant by these terms.

Inspiration, like revelation, is a divine dictate, with the difference that in the second case the Spirit dictates a law-giving and obligatory Message of overriding force, whereas in the first case the Message, whatever be its value, has no dogmatic import, and has an illustrative role within the framework of the fundamental Message.

Reflection, like intellection, is an activity of the intelligence, with the difference that in the second case this activity springs from that immanent divine spark that is the Intellect, whereas in the first case the activity starts from the reason, which is capable only of logic and not of intellective intuition. The *conditio sine qua non* of reflection is that man reason on the basis of data that are both necessary and sufficient and with a view to a conclusion,[1] the latter being the reason for the existence of the mental operation.

From the point of view of knowledge properly so-called, reasoning is like the groping of a blind man, with

---

1. It is precisely the absence of such data that makes modern science aberrant from the speculative point of view, and hypertrophied from the practical point of view; likewise for philosophy: criticism, existentialism, evolutionism, have their respective points of departure in the absence of a datum which in itself is as obvious as it is essential.

the difference that — by removing obstacles — it may bring about a clearing of vision; it is blind and groping due to its indirect and discursive nature, but not necessarily in its function, for it may be no more than the description — or verbalization — of a vision which one possesses *a priori*, and in this case, it is not the mind that is groping, but the language. If we compare reasoning to a groping, it is in the sense that it is not a vision, and not in order to deny its capacity of adequation and exploration; it is a means of knowledge, but this means is mediate and fragmentary, like the sense of touch, which enables a blind man to find his way and even to feel the heat of the sun, but not to see.[2]

As for intellection, on the one hand it necessarily expresses itself by means of reason and on the other hand it can make use of the latter as a support for actualization. These two factors enable theologians to reduce intellection to reasoning; that is to say, they deny it — while at the same time seeing in rationality an element that is more or less problematic if not contrary to faith — without seeking or being able to account for the fact that faith is itself an indirect, and in a way, anticipated mode of intellection.

If on the one hand reasoning can give rise to — but not produce — intellection and if on the other hand intellection is necessarily expressed by reasoning, a third combination is also possible, but it is abnormal and abusive; namely the temptation to support a real intellection by aberrant reasoning; either because the intellection does not operate in all domains on account of some blind spot in the mind or character, or because religious emotivity involves the thought towards solutions stemming from expediency, given that faith is inclined to allow, even if only subconsciously, that "the end sanctifies the means."

In any case, it is impossible to deny that Sufis some-

2. It is said that angels do not possess reason since they have vision of causes and consequences, which obviously does not signify an infirmity.

26

times write "philosophically"—rather than from "inspiration"—especially since the philosopher, far from being a rationalist by definition, is simply a man who reflects on the meaning and causes of phenomena or on the combinations of things, which, after all, is entirely normal for a creature endowed with intelligence but not with omniscience. In another sense, the Sufis reason "theologically" to the extent that they seek to combine an anthropomorphist, moralistic and sentimental monotheism with metaphysics and gnosis, to the detriment of their esoterism; but this particularity plays no role from the point of view of speculative rationality: in this regard there is no strict line of demarcation between philosophy and theology.

*

* *

Another mode of knowledge, if one may put it thus, is the interpretation of sacred Scriptures; in a Semitic context, as one knows, scriptural interpretation, with its play of associations of ideas springing from words or images, often takes the place of thinking. Hermeneutics pertains to inspiration as a prerogative of sanctity, but without for all that being able to dispense with the concurrence of reasoning, nor *a fortiori* of intellection, which it is difficult to separate in practice from inspiration; in any case, it is a peculiarity of inspired interpretation that the starting points of spiritual or mental activity are passages or words from Scripture and not in the first place ideas or intuitions. The fact that the frontier between the supernatural and the natural is not always precise explains the inexhaustible diversity and inequality of Sufic, Shiite and Rabbinical speculations; one has the impression that, with many of these speculations, it is not a question of liberating oneself from cosmic *māyā*, but on the contrary of entrenching oneself more deeply within it; of plunging into religious mythology, with piety and ingenuity, but without the desire to escape from it. Thus the notion of

27

esoterism is fairly precarious in the Semitic monotheistic world, although it is precisely in this world that it is the most necessary;[3] indeed all too often it conveys either a particularly radical and over-refined exoterism, or else an esoterism that is both fragmentary and vulgarized, hence exoterized. "If thou seekest the kernel, thou must break the shell": this maxim, which is as dangerous as it is true, runs the risk of remaining a dead letter in an esoterism conventionally entrenched in dogmatic theology and denominational "mythology." It will no doubt be said that exoterism is the necessary starting point for the corresponding esoterism, which is true insofar as it is a question of pure symbolism, hence open to the universal, and not of exclusivist particularism;[4] due account being taken, obviously, of the need for prudence which in a religious context may distort the dialectic of sapience, and this argument can carry much weight.

Sufism seems to derive its originality, both positive and problematical, from the fact that it mixes, metaphorically speaking, the spirit of the Psalms with that of the *Upanishads*: as if David had sung the *Brahmasūtra*, or as if Bādarāyana had implored the God of Israel. Needless to say this often gives rise to a harmonious, profound and powerful combination, in Ibn 'Atā'illāh for example; as for the drawbacks of this amalgam—which in fact is not an amalgam, since it is spontaneous—one must always take due account of the eschatological idealism which can greatly compensate for pious inconsequences, just as the ardor of faith can compensate for many human imperfections.

3. In Hindu context, Shankarian *Vedānta* is not properly speaking an esoterism since the Rāmānujian perspective, which corresponds to exoterism, does not act as a cover for it, but leads an independent existence.

4. For all the more reason, religious fanaticism cannot be a starting point for gnosis; a truth that Omar Khayyām expressed in his own way.

Christ said two things which are equally plausible, but which at first sight are contradictory: on the one hand, he ordered obedience to the scribes and pharisees, since they are "seated in the chair of Moses," and on the other he described many of their prescriptions as "human"; which means that tradition comprises — or may comprise — elements, which, without departing from "orthodoxy" are, to say the least, unnecessary luxuries and are somtimes harmful to the moral or spiritual essentiality of the Divine Message. These lowering and alienating elements — "human" without being "heterodox" — also exist *de facto* in esoterism, always by virtue of a "human margin" which Heaven concedes to our freedom; it is a question here, not of course of elements which enter directly into the elaboration of sanctity, but of those luxuriant speculations which produce vertigo rather than light.

*

* *

Like the Semites, the Aryans constitute above all a linguistic group, which implies that they also constitute, but more vaguely, a psychological group, and even a racial group, in origin at least; from another point of view, this homogeneity is very relative since the Aryans form but a fragment in a vaster collectivity, namely the white race.[5] Psychologically, there are "introverted" and contemplative Aryans, the Hindus, and "extroverted" and enterprising Aryans, the Europeans; East and West, with the obvious reservation that the characteristics of the one are also to be found in the other. In the case of the Semites, who on the whole are more contemplative than Europeans and less contemplative than Hindus, there are also two principal groups, Jews and Arabs: the soul of the former is richer but more turned in on itself, while that of the

5. This race also comprises the Hamites and the Dravidians, but these groups have far less historical and spiritual importance as the Aryans and the Semites, at least in a direct sense.

29

latter is poorer but more expansive, more gifted from the point of view of radiance and universality.[6]

For the Semite, everything begins with Revelation, and consequently with faith and submission; man is *a priori* a believer and consequently a servant: intelligence itself takes on the color of obedience. For the Aryan on the contrary—and we are not thinking of the Semiticized Aryan[7]—it is intellection that comes first, even if it be kindled thanks to a Revelation; Revelation here is not a commandment which seems to create intelligence *ex nihilo* while at the same time enslaving it, but appears rather as the objectivation of the one Intellect, which is both transcendent and immanent. Intellectual certainty has here priority over obediential faith; the Veda does not give orders to the intelligence, it awakens it and reminds it of what it is.

Grosso modo, the Aryans—except in cases of intellectual obscuration in which they have only retained their mythology and ritualism—are above all metaphysicians and therefore logicians, whereas the Semites—if they have not become idolaters and magicians—are *a priori* mystics and moralists; each of the two mentalities or capacities repeating itself within the framework of the other, in conformity with the Taoist symbol of the *yin-yang*. Or

6. In this comparison, we are thinking of orthodox Jews—those who remained Orientals, even in the West—and not of the totally Europeanized Jews, who combine certain Semitic characteristics with Western extroversion. All the same, Judaism had a certain radiation in the Roman period, but after that, it was indirectly and through Christianity and Islam that the essential monotheistic Message spread, of which Judaism, after Abraham and with Moses, was the first crystallization.

7. It would be a misconception to argue that Al-Ghazālī was Persian, and therefore an Aryan, for the Persians were Arabized by Islam, whether they were Shi'ite or Sunnite; and it goes without saying that a Hellenized Arab is more "Aryan" than an Arabized Persian, schematically speaking. An Iranian or an Indian can be Arabized *a priori* and Hellenized *a posteriori*, and as a result, an Aryanized Semite can be superimposed, in the same person, on a Semiticized Aryan.

again, the Aryans are objectivists, for good or ill, while the Semites are subjectivists; deviated objectivism gives rise to rationalism and scientism, whereas abusive subjectivism engenders all the illogicalities and all the pious absurdities of which sentimental fideism — over-zealous and conventional — is capable. It is the difference between intellectualism and voluntarism; the first tends to reduce the volitive element to the intelligence or to integrate it therein, and the second on the contrary tends to subordinate the intellectual element to the will; this is said without forgetting the fluctuations necessarily comprised in the concrete reality of things. It is sometimes necesary to express oneself in a schematic manner for the sake of clarity if one is to express oneself at all.

*

*   *

The ancient Arabs were both skeptical and superstitious; if they were rationalists, it was because of worldliness, and not because of a shadow of intellectuality; they did not think of putting their rationality, acute though it was, in the service of a truth which in practice was distant and difficult to verify and which in addition seemed to go against their interests; on the contrary, they put it in the service of efficacy, on the plane of magical idolatry as well as on that of commercial enterprises. To drag them away from their indifferentism, it was necessary to cause to vibrate in them a chord other than this completely "horizontal" sagacity; to make them accept a 'vertical" truth, it was necessary to impose on them a simple and enthralling faith, while discrediting a rationality compromised by its pagan character; the man who is converted must "burn what he once adored."

The lasting result of this change is that the pious Moslem is mistrustful of the need for causality in matters of faith; rationality appears to him as a pagan memory and as an invitation to doubt and insubordination, and thus to

31

unbelief; nevertheless, fideism developed its own rationality — dogmatic theology *(kalām)* and the science of the Divine Law *(fiqh)* — but Ghazālī nonetheless considers that on the Day of Resurrection the Imāms of primitive Islam will be hostile to the doctors of the Law, the former having sought only to "please God"; he believes that learned theology is there only to prevent innovations *(bida)*, and that the true knowledge of God is at the antipodes of *kalām*. All this enables us to explain the paradox of an esoterism founded, less on an intellectuality conscious of its nature and its rights than on a voluntaristic, individualistic and sentimental fideism; prolonging exoterism, radicalizing or refining it in a certain way, but only insufficiently perceiving its relativity. Nevertheless we have here the two essential aspects of plenary esoterism: on the one hand the penetration of the symbols of exoterism and on the other hand, on the contrary, the affirmation of the independence — and pre-excellence — of essence with regard to forms, or of substance with regard to accidents, that is, precisely, the formulations of the common religion.[8] As regards this "non-conformist" aspect of esoterism, we would say, by way of illustration, that the abrogations of Koranic verses on the one hand and the matrimonial exceptions in the life of the Prophet on the other hand, are there to indicate respectively the relativity of the formal Revelation and of social morality; which amounts to saying that these abrogations and exceptions pertain to the esoteric perspective, leaving aside their immediate and practical significance.[9]

8. Abū Hurairah: "I kept preciously in my memory two stores of knowledge which I received from the Messenger of God; I passed on one of them, but if I passed on the other, you would cut my throat." One finds a completely analogous passage in the Gospel of St. Thomas. As the Taoists say: "Only error is transmitted, not the truth."
9. This is not unconnected with the mysterious passage which relates the meeting between Moses and *Al-Khidr,* the latter representing, like Melchizedek, supra-formal, universal and primordial spiri-

As for the affinity—in some respects paradoxical and yet fundamental—between Islam and gnosis, it must be pointed out that Islam has the greatest respect for intelligence, in conformity with the Koran and the Sunna, and contrary to what takes place in Christianity, contrary also to the wishes of certain Moslem fideists; but here it is a question of intelligence in itself *('aql)*—which includes the intellect as well as the reason or conversely—and not the intellect alone, which the believer may accept or not accept, depending on his degree of understanding. Intelligence, for the Moslem, is the faculty which allows us to distinguish between what pleases God and leads to salvation and what displeases God and leads to perdition; or between good and evil, true and false, the real and the illusory, in the most elementary sense or in the very highest sense.[10]

---

tuality (*Sura of the Cave,* 65-82). Let us note that the verses abrogated have in general a more universal meaning than the verses which replace them, and that the extra wives—the Koran allowing only four—indicate what one might call the "Krishnaïte" aspect of the Prophet.

10. Traditions advanced by Ghazālī: "The fool does more harm by his ignorance than the wicked man by his wickedness. Furthermore, men will reach a higher degree of nearness *(qurb)* to God only in proportion to their intelligence *('aql* = "intellect")." "Because for everything there is a support, and the support of the believer is his intelligence; his way of worshipping (serving) God (*'ubudiyah* = "servitude") is proportioned to his intelligence." Ghazālī distinguishes in the word *'aql* four meanings: abstract intelligence which distinguishes man from the animals; the instinct of what is possible and impossible; empirical knowledge; discernment of causes and the foreseeing of consequences. "Whoever dies knowing that there is no god but God enters Paradise"; commenting on this *hadīth* in his *Futūhāt al-Makkiyah*—in a section on the modes of *Tawhīd*—Ibn 'Arabī remarks that the Prophet said "Whoever knows" *(ya'lam)* and not "whoever believes" *(yu'min)* nor "whoever says" *(yaqūl)*; and he adds that Iblis also "knew" that there is no god but God, but that he nullified this knowledge by his sin of "association" *(shirk)*. The primacy of "knowledge" is yet a further indication, amongst many others, of the fundamentally "gnostic" nature of Islam.

Sufism: Veil and Quintessence

*

* *

Innumerable detours and endless discourses result from the fact that Sufi metaphysics is linked with the anti-metaphysical and moralizing creationism of the monotheistic theologies, and from the fact that, as a result, it is unable to handle in a sufficiently consequential manner the principle of relativity; radicalism with regard to the essential goes hand in hand with inconsequentiality with regard to detail. No doubt the precautions of theology — metaphysically unnecessary — give rise to perplexities that are fruitful, to the sort of wounds that produce mystical intuitions, but this is unconnected with pure and total truth, to which nevertheless all the Sufists lay claim.

What is it in fact that interests the esoterist, the gnostic, the metaphysician? It is the truth in itself and the intelligence which is proportioned to it: intelligence that is theomorphic, and therefore holy, by the very fact that it is proportioned to the highest truths; holy through its transpersonal root, the "uncreated" and immanent Intellect. And what is it that interests the mystical fideist? It is the sublimizing affirmation of a driving idea, in and through faith; the latter having an almost absolute value by virtue of its dogmatic content on the one hand, and by virtue of its volitive, imaginative and sentimental intensity on the other. From this to believing that one is "inspired" because one abstains from thinking, there is only one step; the fideist is by definition an inspirationist.[11] Admittedly, this tenseness of faith does not exclude intellection properly so-called, but in this case intellection is not the "prime

11. A positive inspiration — the only kind we are envisaging here — can come from God or from an angel, which in practice amounts more or less to the same, but it can also come from the subconscious without for all that being false; nevertheless in this case one is wrong to attribute it without reservation to a heavenly source, although in the last analysis every true intuition can be traced back metaphysically to the one Truth.

34

mover" of the speculations; intellection appears as a gift or
as a concomitance of faith, which is not false since the
Holy Spirit is manifested through the Intellect as well as
through inspirations falling from Heaven. The drawback
is that one attributes to the Holy Spirit, or to inspiration,
the suggestions of pious sentimentality; suggestions which
are not necessarily aberrant, but which may be so.[12]

Jews and Arabs have in common an overflowing
imagination, even when it is poor, which, very paradoxically, is not a contradiction. Many Islamic or more particularly Sufic speculations — without forgetting the Shi'ite
sector — fully rival those rabbinical speculations that are
most subject to caution; it is thus appropriate to take both
cum grano salis and not with the illusion that everything
that lays claim to tradition and comprises a modicum of
sacred science is necessarily infallible.[13] No doubt playing
with complex and exuberant associations of ideas — suggestive both by their content and by their excessiveness —
can procure for the Arab or the Arabized soul a satisfac-
tion that is at least stimulating; but there is not much likelihood that it will have the same effect on other mentalities.[14]

12. From the first centuries of Islam, the preachers *(qāss, qussās)*
sought to strike the imagination of their audience with more or less
extravagant stories in order to stimulate piety, fear, hope; a double-
edged sword if ever there was one, for the result was an inextricable
mixture of the true and the fictitious, and, in the final analysis, a sort
of infantilization of pious literature.

13. A typical problem: can one in certain cases see God with
one's bodily eyes? Were Moses on Sinaï and Mohammed on the occasion of the Night Journey able to see God? Nevertheless, "sight cannot reach Him *(Allāh)*," according to the Koran; and why does one
speak of an "eye of the heart" *('ayn al-qalb)*? For the purpose of the
physical eye is precisely to perceive material things as such, and thus
is not suited to a vision of the immaterial in itself; nor *a fortiori* to a vision of the Archetypes, let alone the Essence. To say that the eye has
seen God is to say that God made Himself form, light, space; or that
the eye has ceased to be eye.

14. Thus the Arab notion of "eloquence" *(balāghah)*, which is not

"There is no right higher than that of Truth," proclaims a princely maxim from India; the monotheists who
stem from the desert—for whom everything commences
with faith—would say rather that there is no right higher
than that of God, or than that of piety. It is perhaps not
too hazardous to say that the Aryan spirit tends *a priori* to
unveil the truth, in conformity with the realism—sacred
or profane—that is proper to it, while the Semitic spirit—
whose realism is more moral than intellectual—tends towards the veiling of the Divine Majesty and of its secrets
that are too dazzling or too intoxicating; as is shown, precisely, by the innumerable enigmas of the monotheistic
Scriptures—in contrast with the *Upanishads*—and as is indicated by the allusive and elliptical nature of the corresponding exegesis.

In any case, it is only too obvious that the great question that arises for man is not to know whether he is Semite or Aryan, Oriental or Western, but to know whether
he loves God, whether he is spiritual, contemplative,
pneumatic; this recalling of the "one thing needful" compensates humanly for what may be unfathomable or trou-
bling in the comparison of spiritual modes.

*

* *

The Arab soul is poor, but heroic and generous; its
poverty as well as its ardor qualify it as a vehicle for a faith
which is centered on the essential—be it a question of doctrine or of worship—and which is all the more passionate
because it is simple. But this poverty, as a psychological
fact, calls forth compensatory features, which are so to
speak "quantitative" by reason of their very poverty;
whence a tendency towards exaggeration and prolixity,
and indeed boastfulness; whence also, on another level, a

unconnected with the deployment, at once ardent, ingenious and pro-
lix, of images and speculations, can give rise to some very diverse
evaluations.

tendency towards contrasting simplification, isolating over-accentuation and too-hasty ostracism; all these features being discernible even in the spiritual literature of the Arabs and those Arabized. Paradoxically, the tendency towards simplification, or towards simplistic alternatives, finds a sort of compensation in allusive and elliptical secretiveness; whence also complication and concealment, detours and veilings.

No doubt the Arab soul has its richness — the contrary would be inconceivable — but it is a poor richness; or a poverty enriched by the scintillation of nomadic virtues, and enhanced by a so to speak desert-like acuteness of intelligence. Nevertheless, in the face of the evidence, one is forced to admit that the exuberance attached to this temperament creates a certain problem from the point of view of sapiential esoterism and its integrity and expression; the thirst for the marvellous is one thing, and metaphysical serenity another.

If there is a poor richness, there is also, and not less paradoxically, a rich poverty, and it is this that predisposed the Arabs to Islam and, along with it, to a mysticism of holy poverty: the saint, in Islam, is the "one who is poor," the *faqīr*, and the spiritual virtue par excellence, which moreover coincides with sincerity *(sidq)*, is "poverty," *faqr*. And without this spirit of poverty, Islam would not have been capable, over a whole section of the globe, of preserving the Biblical world, or of excluding from its universe the literary and artistic and profoundly worldly "culture" of which the West is so proud and from which it is running the risk of dying, if indeed it has not already done so. Those who accuse Islam of "sterility" do not understand that for Islam it is one of the greatest claims to glory that it was able to impress on a whole civilization a certain character of the desert; of holy poverty as well as of holy childhood.[15]

15. A character preserved — or made visible — especially in the Maghrib; we are not speaking of the caliphs of Damascus and Bagh-

Revelation imposes itself on Aryans as on Semites; nonetheless, one is right to speak of an Aryan "intellectionism" and a Semitic "inspirationism," although both intellection and inspiration necessarily belong to all human groups; the entire difference lies in the emphasis. Intellection is sacred because it derives from the Intellect, which pertains to the Holy Spirit; likewise in the case of inspiration, with the difference that it derives from a particular grace and not, as in the case of intellection, from a permanent and "naturally supernatural" capacity.

We do not believe we are over-stylizing things in taking the view that the Aryan tends to be a philosopher,[16] while the Semite is above all a moralist; let us compare, to be convinced of this, the *Upanishads*, the *Yoga-Vasishtha* and the *Bhagavadgītā* with the Bible, or the Hindu doctrines with Talmudic speculations.[17] The innermost mo-

dad nor the Turkish sultans.

16. One might object that the Celtic and Germanic peoples do not answer to this description, at least *a priori*; this would be to forget that the Aryan spirit comprises two dimensions, one mythological and the other intellectual, and that the groups that we have just mentioned put all the emphasis on the mythological and heroic side; not to mention the more than probable existence of an esoteric and oral wisdom, amongst the Germans as well as the Celts.

17. We remarked in one of our first books—and others have since repeated it—that the encounter of Hinduism and Islam on the soil of India has something profoundly symbolic and providential about it, given that Hinduism is the most ancient integral tradition and that Islam on the contrary is the youngest religion; it is the junction of the primordial with the terminal. But there is here more than a symbol; this encounter means in fact that each of these traditions, which are nevertheless as different as possible, has something to learn from the other, not of course from the point of view of dogmas and practices, but from that of tendencies and attitudes; Islam offers its geometric simplicity, its clarity and also its compassion, while Hinduism brings its influence to bear by its profound serenity and by its multiform and inexhaustible universality.

tive of Moslem mysticism is, basically, more moral than intellectual—in spite of the intellective character of the *Shahādah*—in the sense that Arab or Moslem, or Semitic, sensibility always remains more or less volitive, and thus subjectivist, as was noted above; knowledge itself, if it is not envisaged as a gratuitous gift from Heaven, appears almost as a merit of the will, at least *de facto* and in the general context, if not in respect of the deepest intention. To affirm Unity—this is good while being true as well; and the first reason for accepting that God is One seems to be that He has ordered us to believe it. The highest good is therefore to affirm Unity in the most radical and sublime manner possible; this subtly and subconsciously moral instinct seems here to be the stimulus for metaphysical speculation. Also, many concepts resulting from this tendency are not to be taken literally: they are "ideals," in other words schemata intended to inspire an impetus towards Unity; it is the operative intensity of faith that counts here, more than intellectual coherence. It is too easy to object that "esoterism" is beyond even elementary logic, that the "profane" understand nothing of these mysteries and so on; a gratuitous "esoterism" which does not prevent us from sometimes preferring the *'ulamā* "of the outward" *(zāhir)* to the scholars "of the inward" *(bātin)*, or the Hellenizing philosophers to Ghazālī, although we do not fail to recognize the subjective merits of pious extravagances.

It is important to note in this context that the totalitarian accentuation on the Divine Unity in Islam determines and colors the whole perspective, as does, in Christianity, the totalitarian accentuation on the Christ. But whereas in Christianity this conceptual and passional accentuation gives rise firstly to trinitarian absolutism and then to the moral and ascetical cult of the cross, in Islam the accentuation of Unity gives rise to the negation of secondary causes and even of the homogeneity of things, and thus to an occasionalism which in a certain way dismantles the world *ad majorem Dei gloriam*; which, in both cases, singularly removes us from the serene contemplation of the nature of things. Thus there is nothing surprising in the fact that thought, which in Christianity always tends toward the "fact" since Christ is a historical phenomenon, in Islam will readily display an occasionalist, and therefore discontinuous coloration, which partly explains certain paradoxical features of Moslem mysticism, beginning with an inspirationism that cares little for coherence.

And this leads to the following parenthesis: whereas the Bible is a book that is directly historical and indirectly doctrinal, the Koran is a book that is directly doctrinal and indirectly historical; in other words, in the Koran, which seeks only to proclaim the Unity, Omnipotence, Omniscience and Mercy of God and correlatively the existential, moral and spiritual servitude of man, historical facts are only points of reference and have scarcely any interest in themselves. This is why the Prophets are quoted without any chronological order and why historical occurrences are sometimes related so elliptically as to be unintelligible without commentaries; the fact is that only the relationship Lord-servant is of importance here, the rest being but illustration or symbolism. A comparison between the Old Testament and the Koran has no meaning apart from these considerations; as for the New Testament, it combines the two styles—it is eminently historical and at the same time explicitly doctrinal—but it has the peculiarity, as compared with the Koran, that it presents different levels of inspiration, as is likewise the case with the Old Testament. The Moslem reproach of "falsification" of the Scriptures no doubt refers to these differences, in an indirect and symbolic manner and with an ostracism that is in no wise exceptional in the realm of exoteric oppositions.

As is indicated by the Testimony of Faith, the *Shahādah*, Islam is the religion of Divinity as such—not of Divine Manifestation, as is Christianity—and by way of consequence, of the conformity of the human "form" to the divine "Essence"; as is indicated, in its turn, by the second *Shahādah*, that of the Prophet. In relation to the evidentness of the Divine Principle, all the other things evident and certain and all the miracles in the world are but little; whence the profound and almost explosive conviction of the Moslem, and his passionate faith, a faith that is at the same time necessarily serene through its very object; this complementarity indicating in addition a certain choice, depending on the level of the doctrine or of the soul.

Islam's conviction that, as religion, it is both quintessence and synthesis, namely that it is the religion that offers everything that constitutes the essence of every possible religion, is certainly not unfounded; for firstly, Islam affirms — to the point of being almost reducible to this affirmation — that there is but one sole Absolute, which is both Unique and Total; secondly it affirms that the universal Law — the *Dharma* as the Hindus would say — is the conformity of contingent beings to the Absolute, and this is what is expressed by the term *Islām*, "Abandonment," "Submission" or "Resignation"; thirdly, the essence of salvation is the recognition — or the awareness — of the Absolute and nothing else; fourthly, Islam teaches that the link between the Absolute and the contingent, or between God and the world, is that God periodically sends Messengers to remind men of the two fundamental truths, that of the Absolute and that of Conformity to the Absolute: *Allāh* and *Islām*; all this having of necessity to be prefigured in the personal nature of the Prophet, in conformity with the congeniality and complementarity between the sacred content and the providential container. This concise summary we consider to be of decisive importance.

*

* *

41

From the doctrinal point of view, the Sufis seek, consciously or otherwise, to combine two tendencies, Platonism and Asharism.[18] Whereas for Platonism, as for all true metaphysics, the true, the beautiful and the good are such because they manifest qualities proper to the Principle, or to the Essence if one prefer, and because God, though supremely free, cannot be free in opposition to His nature which He obviously cannot change except on pain of absurdity — while such is the case for all true metaphysics, we say, Asharism on the contrary proclaims that the true, the beautiful and the good are such because God wills it so, without our being able to know why, and that the contrary could be the case if by chance God so willed. In this system, which is voluntaristic because it is viscerally moralistic and therefore individualistic, God and man are defined as will: God as "absolutely free" will, capable of determining things no matter how and for no other reason than it is His will, as if will had its sufficient reason in itself, and as if freedom could logically and ontologically include the absurd; correlatively, man is defined as will predestined for obedience, and apparently free in its choices "if God wills." Obviously Sufism, on this battlefield, approaches pure gnosis to the extent that it is Platonic — which does not mean that sound doctrine necessarily comes to it from Plato or Plotinus — and it departs from it to the extent that it capitulates to Asharism. According to "ontological monism" *(wahdat al-wujūd)*, everything that exists is "good" because "willed by God"; the notion of evil is in our minds because "God willed it"; evil is what we do not love, or what *a priori* God does not love. We are not told why God does not love certain things, even though all things are good "in themselves"; we must take note of the fact that He does not love them, and this

18. The same phenomenon moreover, occurred within Christianity, the Asharite tendency being here replaced by evangelical fideism; the combination with, and opposition to, Platonism, go side by side.

constitutes all our "knowledge." Here the most vertigi-
nous metaphysics is combined with the most summary
Asharism.

Be that as it may, the "Platonic" thesis is expressed in
the Koran not only by the formula "in the Name of God,
the Clement, the Merciful," but also by all other formulas
enunciating the aspects or qualities of God and thus af-
firming the immutable and at the same time intelligible
character of the divine nature; if 'Asharī did not draw
from this the fundamental consequences which impose
themselves, it is because of his immanent moralism—
which doubtless coincides with moral and social opportuneness.

*

* *

"God doeth what He will," says the Koran, and it is
the only thing that 'Asharī seems to remember, at least in
a consequential fashion; he forgets that other Koranic
verses implicitly proclaim that "God doeth what He is":
which occurs, for example, when God carries out justice
because He is the Just *(al-Hakīm)*, or when He produces
beauty because, according to a *hadīth*, He is beautiful
(jamīl) and loves beauty; or again when he forgives because He is always by His very nature, "He who for-
giveth" *(al-Ghafūr)*. God cannot possess the freedom of not
being what He is, and consequently, of not manifesting it;
all the emphasis in reality is on the Divine Being and not
on Will. God is not *a priori* "Will," He is Perfection; and
thus all possible perfections. He is free in the play of possibilities, but not in respect of their essences, which pertain to Divine Possibility as such; the imperatives of Possibility take precedence over this play just as Being takes
precedence over things.

According to Asharite reasoning, God is free to "do
what He will" because there is no one above Him; the
good is the good, not by virtue of an intrinsic quality di-

43

rectly reflecting a given aspect of the Divine Perfection, but for the sole reason that God willed it thus; here the error is, on the one hand confusing Omnipotence, or All-Possibility, with the arbitrary, and on the other hand forgetting that the foundation of the good is, not a decree from God, but the intrinsic goodness of the Divine Nature. If two and two are four, this is true because God is Truth, and not because He is Omnipotence or gratuitousness.

Be that as it may, Islam had either to teach like Mazdeism that there are two "divinities," one for good and one for evil—an idea which emphasizes contingency and not Absoluteness, except for the final Victory—or to proclaim that "God doeth what He will"; which, instead of being interpreted "in an ascending direction," in the sense of All-Possibility and the difference of cosmic planes, has all too often been interpreted "in a descending direction," in the sense of an arbitrariness which obviously excludes the Divine Perfection. Whoever emphasizes the side of contingency, manifestation, world, must veil the Absolute, which is what Mazdean dualism did, and likewise in a less abrupt fashion Christian trinitarianism; whoever, on the contrary, emphasizes the Absolute—still keeping to the level of a religious voluntarism—cannot help "veiling" in a certain manner the side of contingency by too unilaterally reducing its workings to the Transcendent Cause; as is shown precisely, in Islam, by a certain "atomizing" and occasionalist unintelligibility of the world. This dilemma arises for the dogmatic formulation, and not for pure metaphysics which has the benefit of a suppleness or a mobility that dogmatism cannot achieve; thus the role of esoterism is to surmount dogmatist disequilibriums and not to prolong or refine them.

Ibn 'Arabī, in spite of his unevennesses and contradictions—the latter being due above all to his at least partial solidarity with common theology, and also with the discontinuous, isolating, and over-accentuating quality of its thought—had the great merit of enunciating the mystery of radiating and inclusive Unity in a fully Asharite environment, and thus of putting the emphasis on the implicitly divine character of cosmic Manifestation, which brings us back to pure and integral metaphysics; it is in this, and not in his more or less expeditive argumentations, nor in his "mythological" imagination, nor in his mystical outbursts, that the whole significance of his work resides. Along with this merit goes that of having put the Platonic love of the Beautiful at the summit of the universal hierarchy, of having discerned it in God Himself and of having replaced—but without abolishing—the God-as-Will of 'Ashari by God-as-Beauty or God-as-Love.[19]

This equation signifies for us that the Absolute by definition comprises Infinitude, in which precisely are rooted, and from which, consequently, are derived, all beauty and all love; so much so that it is the beauty and the love perceived in the world that enable us to have the presentiment, and even to actualize within ourselves, what the radiant nature of God is.[20]

*

* *

The distinction between the necessary and the possible, which concerns all domains of the universe, applies

19. Mention must also be made of the fundamental doctrine of "Universal Man" *(al-Insān al-kāmil)*, which is the Logos that prefigures the created universe; it is reflected—or is realized existentially—in the microcosm as well as in the macrocosm, and it is also especiallly manifested in the Prophets and the Sages; the Prophets are summarized in the person of the Founder of Islam. This theory derives its justification and its inspiration from the theomorphism of man.

20. It can be said that Love, together with Beauty, Goodness and Beatitude, is a mystery of a "dimension" of the Essence, but not that the Essence is nothing other than Love; as Absolute, the Essence is ineffable, and it also manifests its nature precisely by Spirit and by Power. It is *Sat, Chit, Ananda;* in Arabic: *Wujūd,* "Reality" (or *Qudrah,* "Power"), *Shuhūd,* "Perception" (or *Hikmah,* "Wisdom"), *Hayāt* "Life" (or *Rahmah,* "Generous, Merciful Goodness").

45

notably to the domain of thought and activity as well, and in particular to that of mystical inspiration. Hence there are necessarily, alongside inspirations pertaining to the necessary or the certain, others that pertain only to the possible and the uncertain; and there are still others that are illusory without for all that being harmful; religious enthusiasm, coupled with a thirst for information about heavenly things and also with an almost conventional over-estimation of religious mythology as such, cannot but give rise to a margin of dreams, not to say illusions. Also, Christian theology rightly teaches that such mirages are not opposed to sanctity as long as they are simply human and not diabolic;[21] it is appropriate to remember this when confronted with pious fantasies on the margin of the love of God and a heroical virtue.[22]

Thus, there is a Sufism which is necessary and another which is possible, just as there is a necessary Being and possible existences; the first of these Sufisms is founded on the esoteric evidences that result from the immutable elements of Islam, whereas the second pertains to personal inspirations, philosophico-mystical speculations, religious mythology, hagiography, zeal and morality.

It can be seen from numerous Sufi treatises that Moslems like to present metaphysical truths, to the extent possible, in terms of subjective experience, whereas Hindus

21. There is a rather large number of mystics whom the Church has canonized without for all that ratifying all their experiences and opinions. More or less innocent inspirationist illusions are possible in particularly imaginative devotees, who are not thereby false mystics and who may even be saints, and possibly valid philosophers, depending on the case.

22. Rūmī attributes to God the following discourse: "What matter words to me? I need an ardent heart; let the hearts become inflamed with love and occupy thyself neither with thoughts nor their expression." This is said in order to excuse human weakness, but not to excuse wisdom; it is at that same time a reference to the mystical unanimity of the religions.

for example present these truths in pure objectivity, as if the subject did not exist, which seems paradoxical when one thinks of the transcendent subjectivism of the *Vedānta;* it is true that Moslems do the same in those of their treatises that are neoplatonic in style—these treatises always having a Koranic or Mohammedian basis—but the most general expression of Sufism unquestionably has the subjectivist character which we have just indicated; in other words, the stages towards transcendent Reality are presented less as objective and immutable "envelopes of the Self" than in their aspect as "moral stations," in the widest and deepest sense that one can give to this epithet. The "states" *(ahwāl)* and "stations" *(maqāmāt)* of Sufism are in principle innumerable and their description is governed by the way of the author, which does not alter the fact that, on the one hand, these experiences clearly possess a character of perfect objectivity as points of reference, otherwise it would be pointless to speak of them, or that on the other hand—and this must again be stressed—Islam possesses a metaphysical and cosmological doctrine expressed in objective terms, founded on the Koran and the Sunna and occasionally influenced, in its conceptualization, by the categories of Hellenistic esoterism.

But in Islam, spirituality properly so-called, always retains its solidarity with the "objective subjectivism" of faith—and thus with the sincerity of faith and with the inward virtues determined by unitary Truth—of which the Koran and the Sunna are the paradigms; the originality of Sufism is that it presents itself as a metaphysics of the human virtues which are inherent in faith or let us say, in the consciousness of the Absolute, and which in the last analysis are rendered supernatural by this very inherence.

The distinction between the "possible" and the "necessary" in Sufism leads us to formulate, or recall, the following point: esoterism is without a country and it establishes itself wherever it can. Historical Sufism is *grosso modo* a sector of the exoterism in which esoterism has found refuge; esoterism is not like the branch of a tree, but like mistletoe, descended from Heaven and placed on the branch; and this association justifies the assertion in general terms that Sufism is esoterism. We do not say, therefore, that this equation is wrong, we say that it is approximate and sufficient for everyday language; and this is all the more true in that the esoteric tendency in any case comprises degrees.

*

* *

The presence of the element "intoxication" *(sukr)* at the heart of Islam—but then we find ourselves in compensatory esoterism and in *bhakti*—is all the more paradoxical in that Islam is indirectly aware of the disequilibrizing element which *de facto* is comprised within Christianity, for better and for worse: in fact, the Renaissance, betrayal though it was, would never have taken hold if it had not profitted from a reaction against an idealism of the hereafter—contemptuous of an accursed here-below—which weighed upon souls and bodies in an unrealistic and disproportionate fashion. To the accursed "natural" reality, anathematized by an isolated and apparently hostile "supernatural" reality, Islam means to oppose a sacralized and thereby supernaturalized "natural"; which it could not realize except at the cost of some excesses, in conformity with the ineluctable principle of the "human margin." Islam senses in Christianity a kind of "wine," and the prohibition of intoxicating beverages is in a sense parallel to the rejection of the penitential idealism that characterizes Christianity; intrinsically speaking, this prohibition runs parallel to the affirmation of a point of view of equilibrium or stability, and thus of the integration of the virtualities of disequilibrium.[23]

23. During the "Night Journey" *(Laylat al-Mi'rāj),* the Archangel

48

Still on the subject of "wine" or "intoxication," it is useful to note that one of the most authentic expressions of Moslem esoterism is the dance of the dervishes, which has as its basis, not the elaborations of theology, but either the Names *Allāh* or *Huwa* ("He"), or the *Shahādah*—symbol of all faith and all metaphysics—combined with the mystery of the Heart and consequently with the mystery of Union. The theme of this dance, like that of the *Dhikr* in general and in the final analysis even of all sacred art, is the return of the accidents to the Substance: in other words art in general and the dance in particular express the Substance which has become accident, and it is from this origin that spring forth the beauty, the profundity and the power of accident-symbols; art expresses this relationship in a movement that is both descending and ascending since on the one hand it reveals the Archetype in the form and on the other hand brings back the form, or the soul, to the Archetype.[24]

The return of the accidental to the Substance, of the formal to the Essence,[25] amounts to the reintegration of plurality into Unity; now Unity, which in the geometrical

Gabriel let the Prophet choose between three beverages: water, wine and milk; the Prophet chose milk, which here symbolizes equilibrium or the happy medium. Even the Koranic style can be explained by this rejection both of the water and the wine: that is to say of a logician's transparency felt to be too "easy" and irreverent, and of a mystical musicality too enthralling and thus too dangerous; an observation that is valid at least for the general style of the Koran, which is both dry and sibylline, but also endowed with a virile rhythm.

24. What constitutes the falseness of extra-traditional art is that it is wont to express the accidentality of accidents, thereby losing its entire reason for existence; except the completely negative reason of accidentalizing souls and minds and thus of making them outward and worldly.

25. The difference between the two expressions is that, in the case of the Substance, there is continuity—even though conditional—whereas in the case of the Essence, there is discontinuity, and thus a "leap into the void"; this is the whole difference between concentric circles and the cross.

order is equivalent to the point, comprises in reality and as if by compensation a mystery of dilation, exactly as the Absolute by definition comprises Infinitude; perfect concentration coincides with an "expansion of the breast" *(inshirāh)*, whence the name *dhikr as-sadr* ("invocation by the breast") that is sometimes given to the dance of the dervishes.

This dance pertains, like sexual life, to a magic that is at once vital, existential and sacramental; it symbolically transfers the finite into the Infinite, or the "I" into the Self, in a virtual manner yet at the same time effective on its psychological plane. Other dances have the function of evoking a cosmic genius, that of love, for example or that of war; the sacred dance, for its part, does not tend to such and such an essence, it tends towards the Essence as such. It tends thereto in principle and under the veil of less absolute, but always interiorizing, intentions: virtually bringing back form to Essence, it prefigures the mystery of union, the mystical miracle which makes the drop become the sea.[26]

Christians readily reproach these types of practice for their "easiness" and their "artificial" character, but this is because Westerners rarely have the sense of the metaphysical transparency of phenomena and because they insist by preference on penitential means; this is the point of view of the moral alternative, not that of contemplative participation in the Archetype by means of the symbol, or in the Essence by means of the form. Nevertheless there have always been in Europe popular dances, in spite of the ill humor of the religious authorities, and it is probable that they were not always profane, especially those of the month of May; that is to say, sacred intentions in

---

26. Rūmī: "In the rhythms of music a secret is hidden: if I were to divulge it, it would overturn the world." Like Chaitanya, Rumi had "chosen the way of dance and music," among the "roads that lead to God."

varying degrees, inherited from Nordic or Mediterranean antiquity, may have found refuge in them.[27]

*

* *

As it is in the nature of esoterism to recognize the essence—which by definition is one—in all forms either religious or sapiential, and consequently to be tolerant, as far as is practically possible, one may be surprised to find in the Sufis not only denominational narrowness but also intolerance; mere lack of information in many cases, and yet lack of spiritual imagination in others, and an inconsistency with regard to the principle of essentiality and universality. Even when such is not the case, one has to welcome declarations of universality with prudence, for it can happen that they also embrace idolators, so that one does not know whether the "tolerance" has in view formulated religions or simply a sort of underlying and unconscious natural religion, which refers to the Divinity as everything does; in the latter case, the attestation of universality is meant to testify to the loftiness of spirit of the Sufi and not to the validity of other religions. Moreover, such declarations are sometimes followed by passages establishing the supremacy of Islam, which cannot be explained simply by reasons of prudence, for if one must fear the 'ulamā to such an extent, it would be better not to speak of universality; unless it be a question here of a kind of dividing of the mind as in the case of the "double truth" of the Christian Middle Ages, in which case it is difficult to know where to place the accent, or to what degree the line of demarcation is clear.

27. In Judaism, the dance of Miriam and that of David left a concrete memory; whence the persistance down to our own day of the dance that is either liturgical, or properly mystical: a dance of triumph after the crossing of the "Red Sea" of the passions and a dance of joy before the Divine Presence, the *Shekhina*, actualized firstly by the "Ark of the Covenant," then by the Holy-of-Holies in the Temple and later, in the diaspora, by the *Sepher Torah*.

The question that arises here *a priori* is the following, and it is both banal and enigmatic: why are religions and theologies not tolerant of other religions and theologies.[28] This intolerance is often regarded as a needless and regrettable luxury, and it is so regarded by ignorant esoterists as well as by profane idealists; in reality, it is the only possible means of protection against errors, for if it is assumed that a religion could proclaim that salvation can also come from the outside, how could this religion still reject false masters presenting themselves in the name of a personal revelation? If religion is intolerant, it will no doubt exclude many foreign values, but as it offers everything that man has need of in view to his final ends, the evil is in practice very relative; whereas if it is tolerant it opens the door to the lethal poisons of pseudo-spiritualisms, without the values of the foreign religions offering the slightest help. This is to say that intolerance is merely an extreme simplification of the self-protection necessary for every spiritual form, hence a kind of preventive war against all possible counterfeits and corruptions; now it is infinitely more important for a religion to keep intact its truths and spiritual means, which are certain and in practice sufficient, than to open itself to foreign values at the risk of losing its own.

As for esoterism, it is necessarily open, in principle, to all intrinsically orthodox forms, but it compensates this openness and the dangers that it may comprise with criteria proper to itself which are all the more rigorous and which in fact are beyond the reach of exoterism; the latter has no need of them, precisely, since its nature permits it to simplify the question *a priori*. The intrinsic truth obviously has priority over the problem of its possible forms; metaphysics, combined with human experience, obliges

28. Not necessarily with regard to a particular philosophy, since philosophies are hardly ever presented with religious requirements; if they are, they are either denominational theories, or particularly harmful human inventions.

us nonetheless to accept the diversity of the forms of the one Truth.[29]

Among the statements made by Ibn 'Arabī about the universality of truth and so about the "religion of the heart," the most explicit — and the one most directly in conformity with the esoteric perspective — is doubtless the following, which comes from the *Fusūs al-Hikam*: "The believer . . . only praises the Divinity comprised within his belief (such as it is comprised therein) and it is to this that he is attached; he cannot perform any act that does not revert to him (its author) and likewise he cannot praise anything without thereby (in effect) praising himself. For without doubt, to praise the work is only to praise its au-

---

29. In principle — although the hypothesis is excluded for more than one reason — the Christ could have said that Hinduism is a form of truth, but he could not have enumerated all the Hindu heresies existent in his time, nor all the heresies still to come; and so on for all the religions. It sufficed him to say that He Himself is the Truth, which is absolutely certain and which in practice is sufficient for a given human cosmos or for given predestined men. In his *Tarjumān al-Ashwāq*, Ibn 'Arabī sings: "My heart has become receptive to every form . . . a temple for idols, a kaaba for a Moslem pilgrim, the tablets of the Torah and the book of the Koran. I adhere to the religion of love . . . " All religious forms, Ibn 'Arabī comments, unite in the love of God, and yet: "No religion is more excellent than the one founded on the love — and the need — of God . . . This religion of love is the prerogative of the Moslems; for the station of the most perfect love has been imparted to the Prophet Mohammed exclusively, and not to the other prophets; for God accepted him as his well-beloved friend." The extenuating circumstance for this abrupt and unintelligible denominationalism is the fact that for each religion, the Prophet who founded it is the sole personification of the total, and not the partial, Logos; however, one might expect an esoterist not to enclose himself in this concept-symbol, but to make mention, since he has opted for the essence, of the relativity of forms — even those that are dear to him — and to do so in an objective and concrete, and not merely metaphorical manner; or else to remain silent, out of pity. But we are obliged to take note of the *de facto* existencce of two esoterisms, one partially formalistic and the other perfectly consistent; all the more so as the facts cannot always be at the level of the principles.

thor; beauty, like lack of beauty, reverts to the author (of the work). The divinity in whom one believes is (so to speak) fashioned by he who conceives *(nādhir)*, it is therefore (in this respect) his work; the praise addressed to what he believes is praise addressed (indirectly and with regard to conceptualization) to himself. And this is why he (the believer insofar as he limits God) condemns every belief except his own: if he were just, he would not do this; but he does it because, fixed on a particular object of worship *(al-ma'būd al-khass)*, he is beyond all doubt in ignorance; and this is why his belief in God implies the negation of everything that is other than it. If he knew what Junayd said — that the color of the water is the color of the vessel — he would allow every believer (whose belief is other than his own) to believe what he (the other believer) believes; he would know God in every form and in every object of belief. But he (the man limited by his belief) follows his opinions without having (total) knowledge and that is why God said (through a *hadīth qudsī*): I conform to the opinion that my servant forms of Me *('inda dhanni 'abdī bī)*. That is to say, I only appear to him in the form of his belief; if he will, let him expand *(atlaqa)* (his conception of Me), and if he will, let him constrict it *(qayyada)*. The Divinity in which one believes assumes the limits (of the belief), and this is the Divinity which (according to a *hadīth qudsī*) the heart of the slave contains; the absolute Divinity not being contained in anything since it is the essence of things as well as its own essence . . . " It is important to understand here that the image of the "believer who praises himself" must be applied above all — according to the logic of things — to a given religious point of view and by this fact to a given believing collectivity; further, that the fact of thus praising "oneself" does not exclude — obviously since one cannot do otherwise — that at the same time and above all one praises God; not such and such a conception of God, but through it the Divinity in itself.

It results from all these considerations that God is the

same for all the religions only in the Divine "strato-sphere," and not in the human "atmosphere"; in the latter, each religion has practically its own God, and there are as many Gods as there are religions. In this sense it could be said that esoterism alone is absolutely monotheistic, it alone recognizing only one religion under diverse forms. For, if it is true that the form, in a certain manner, "is" the essence, the latter on the contrary is in no wise the form; the drop is water, but water is not the drop.

*

*   *

The fact that man tends to conceive in his own image what he worships, is shown equally by the various levels of piety within the same religious collectivity; but here more than ever we must be careful not to attribute to God the limitations of men. To be sure, God accepts the particular piety of the pedantic, or the excessively servile soul, but not as an accomplice or a despot; otherwise He would not respond to intelligence, or nobility, which pierce the fog of a limited mentality.[30] God can assuredly love littleness insofar as it is weak, simple, trusting and touching; He cannot love in it any possible aspects of pettiness or opacity. Moreover — and confusions are frequent on this plane — God hates pridefulness, but not a justified self-respect; hypocrisy, but not a dignity that is natural and inherent in the sense of the sacred; profane and impertinent curiosity, but not the need for causality that is part of understanding. God demands humility, but not necessarily modesty; sincerity, but not cynicism, even well-intentioned;[31] obedience, but not servility insofar as it takes away from man what God has granted him. And

30. Every mentality as such comprises limits, but it is of particular, and not general and existential, limitations that we speak of here.
31. As in the case of the *malāmatiyah*, who through sincerism "show the bad and hide the good."

55

above all: God is sovereignly free, without His Freedom giving rise to arbitrariness; He is Necessary Being, without His Necessity implying the least constraint. "God doeth what He will": this Koranic expression means above all that God is what He is.

CHAPTER 3

Paradoxes of an Esoterism

A Sufi author was able to write without hesitation that the supreme state, with regard to which every other state is but a veil *(hijāb)* and a drawing away *(b'ud)*, is that there is no longer any place in one's consciousness for any created thing and in so saying, he is not speaking of ecstasy, he means it with regard to man's habitual state, as if this were not to ruin the very notion of the human being or of the creature as such, and as if any saint, beginning with the Prophet himself, had ever shown an example of such a sublimity, which in fact is as impossible as it is unnecessary. This sublimity nevertheless offers an "ideal" image, which is very suggestive in its fashion of union with God; this we concede, in taking account of temperaments that are sensitive to this type of hyperbolism. It seems to us in any event that it would have been more realistic to say: when man absents himself from the world for God, God makes himself present in the world for man; but man, were he the greatest saint, does not cease to perceive things; he does not see God in their place, but he sees them "in God" and they communicate to him "something of God."

Another example of an excessive dialectic — one to which we have already referred — is the following: a certain Sufi author affirms that everything is good because everything that exists is willed by God, but feels obliged to conclude that evil is only a matter of perspective. The author of this thesis and his partisans are right to say that everything is good through pure existence and through the positive qualities superimposed on it,[1] but not to subjectivize evil; not to see that evil is due to the remoteness necessitated by cosmogonic radiation and that evil manifests precisely privation of the good, and thus marks the absence of the Sovereign Good. We have seen above that a certain kind of monism thinks it can subjectivize evil, not only in the case of creatures, but even in the case of God: evil, it is said, is what God does not like; this is logic in reverse, and is explained by a pious concern not to make divine attitudes depend on external causes and always to leave the initiative or the *primum mobile* to the Divinity; as if it were not sufficient to state that there are phenomena which are contrary to the Divine Prototype — not in their ontological necessity but in their simple phenomenality — and that God is opposed to them on the plane where this opposition has a meaning.

On a completely different level, but in the same category of excessive speculations, is the following example: when the patriarch Joseph made himself known to his brothers and the latter prostrated themselves before him, he remembered his prophetic dream — the sun and the moon and eleven stars bowing down before him[2] — and he made the following remark, according to the Koran: "This is the interpretation of my dream of old, that my Lord has made real." Quoting this impeccable passage in his *Fusūs* (chapter *Kalimah Yūsufiyah*), Ibn 'Arabī thinks it necessary to introduce the *hadīth*: "People are asleep (during their lives), and when they die, they wake up"; in other words, he takes the opportunity to declare that Joseph did not know this truth, and he does so in order to conclude that Mohammed was wiser: "See then how excellent are the knowledge and the rank of Mohammed!"

1. This moreover is St. Augustine's theory.
2. The Islamic tradition does not seem to have retained the other dream, that of the sheaves of Joseph's brothers bowing down before Joseph's sheaf.

he says to the reader. Question: how can one believe for an instant that Joseph, having the quality of Prophet, did not know that earthly life is a dream, and that death is an awakening; and even if he did not have this quality, how can one prove, by referring to the words quoted—which concern a particular fact and not a principle—that he did not know the truth expressed by the *hadīth* in question? Moreover, a Vedantist might make the point—without any Sufi rushing to exalt his "knowledge" or his "rank"— that the beyond is likewise but a dream and the awakening is only in the Absolute; or again, that the *jīvan-mukta* has realized this supreme awakening without having had to pass through bodily death, and that this is therefore not the condition *sine qua non* of the ultimate awakening. Finally, if the realization of Joseph's dream is not the homage of his brothers, what then is it, and how does Ibn 'Arabī envisage a realization of this dream in the beyond? And this not to mention the fact that, according to the Koran, it is God Himself who taught Joseph the interpretation of dreams.[3]

One may think that, in writing these lines of the *Fusūs*, Ibn 'Arabī wished to acquit himself of a duty of piety towards the Prophet: to speak well of him, to miss no opportunity for doing so, even to the detriment of other Messengers. When reading passages of this kind, one must in fact take account of the following principle of Moslem piety: it is morally beautiful to seize every opportunity to speak well of the Prophet, no matter how, but on condition that one does not say that he is the son of God. Thus,

---

3. Moreover, if Joseph's knowledge was imperfect and if it was because of this imperfection that he remembered his dreams when he saw his brothers prostrate themselves before him, his knowledge was also imperfect when he explained their dreams to his two companions in prison and then to the king. According to this opinion, every interpretation of premonitory dreams would have to be reduced to the idea that death is their only realization, and this empties the very notion of "interpretation" *(ta'wīl)* of all its content.

59

when speaking of the other Messengers, it is not a question of defining them, it is uniquely a question of making use of their names to shore up the scale of values proper to Islam. All the same, one has the right to expect a more nuanced and more objective perspective in an esoteric context.

In an analogous order of ideas, not as far as we know in Ibn 'Arabī, but in his favorite disciple Sadr ad-Dīn Qūn-yawī, we find a reference to the following story, traces of which are also to be found in Attar, in his *Mantiq at-Tayr* as well as in his *Elahi Nameh*: Christ, at the moment of his ascension, was stopped at the threshold of the fourth Heaven by angels who examined him and, having found a pin in his clothing, prevented him from ascending further; or, according to another version, prevented him from so doing until he rid himself of the pin. We suppose that in its fundamental intention this extravagant story is directed at Christian theology insofar as it divinizes Jesus and reduces God to a Trinity—insofar as it "christifies" God, if one so prefer—but in fact it implicates the very person of Christ, and there is little likelihood that the average reader will guess the polemical intention which we have mentioned hypothetically, and which would constitute an attenuating circumstance, dogmatic oppositions being what they are.[4] Falling within this same category of story-making lacking a sense of proportion as well as a sense of the ridiculous—and in which poverty of imagination is readily combined with a desire not to be outdone—we find from the pen of Attar, Qūnyawī and other authors the anecdote about the Archangel Gabriel who, seeking to accompany the Prophet on the occasion of the "Night Journey" right up to the presence of God, was stopped by the scissors of the "no" (*lā*) of the *Shahādah*,

---

4. A rather relative attenuating circumstance as far as the Prophet is concerned, for very often, if not always, the Mahometology of the Sufis amounts in practice to a divinization.

which cut a hundred thousand feathers from his wings;[5] only the Prophet having the right and the capacity to go on to the end.

Amongst exegetes, there is an incurable breed who always know better and who always insist on dotting the i's; in short, who always know everything. When the Koran tells us that God, on seeing Abraham thrown into the flames, gave them the order: "Be cold," the exegetes in question know better what actually occurred: the Archangel Gabriel brought a celestial tunic which protected Abraham against the fire. And when, three generations later, Joseph sent his tunic to his father who had become blind and who recovered his sight on contact with this garment, our commentators know better: it was not Joseph's tunic, it was Abraham's, inherited by Joseph; as if the tunic of Joseph, prophet and patriarch, would not have sufficed to bring about the miracle, and as if the symbolism of the story did not require that Jacob, having become blind because of his having wept for Joseph, should be healed precisely by Joseph; and as if Joseph could have inherited something as precious as Abraham's tunic when — apart from Benjamin — he was the youngest of eight brothers, and what brothers! It is just as improbable that the latter, on throwing Joseph naked into the well, should have let him keep the miraculous tunic;[6] then that the slave merchants and later the Egyptians should have left it with him. Be that as it may, the Koran relates without any ambiguity the following words of Joseph: "Take this my tunic; apply it to my father's face; he will recover his sight . . . ": "My tunic" and not "Abraham's tunic."[7] Without being pedantic or perfectionistic one

5. *Lā ilāha illā 'Llāh*: "No divinity except God *(Allāh)* (alone)." In Arabic script the word *lā* resembles a pair of scissors.

6. Enclosed in a small bag attached to his neck, it seems, which must have made a fairly bulky object; we are asked to believe that the young man always carried it beneath his clothing.

7. Omar Suhrawardī, although a great theologian, turns to this

61

may consider that while an interpretation can have the function of completing a literal ellipsis, it does not, on the contrary, have the right to seek to correct and contradict a perfectly clear and sufficient text.

Still in the realm of pious onesidedness and disproportion, but on a less blameworthy level, tradition or legend attributes to the Prophet—not by inventing them but by presenting them as principles and by remaining silent about complementary features[8]—acts of goodness which would have been impracticable in any circumstance; less on the part of the Prophet than with regard to the people who would have benefitted from them, and who could not all have been saints capable of bearing such solicitude without abusing it. What the chroniclers seem to forget, is that a kindness must be proportioned to those who receive it—or inversely, that the virtue of those who receive it must be proportioned to the kindness—and that a sense of proportion, according to the Koran itself, is a virtue just as much as generosity; and that it is, to say the least, misplaced to attribute to a man qualities—or rather the application of qualities—which are foreign to God, which

story when he speaks of the patched robe *(muraqqa'ah)* of the Sufis, and even mentions the chain of those who passed it on. Once again, we do not contest that such stories may contain a symbolism that can even be profound, but they are nonetheless absurd in their materiality. It is true that the absurdity can itself indicate a purely symbolic intention, which would be a sufficient explanation if the end always justified the means. Be that as it may, in the story quoted everything is explained when it is accepted that it is a question of an Abrahamic charisma inherited only by Joseph, namely a bodily radiance that was both protective and healing; but this has no connection with the patched clothing of the Sufis, which indicates poverty, not glory; the earthly, not the heavenly.

8. According to Al-Ghazālī and others, the Prophet never became angry; one certainly does not expect so much of him. Moses and Jesus showed holy anger; how can one believe that Mohammed —an Arab and a warrior—never did so? 'Aisha reports that the soul of the Prophet was like the Koran; now the Koran expresses anger, by informing us—and assuring us—of the Wrath of God.

shows precisely that they are the products of a moral idealism and not concrete modes of behavior.

Admittedly, the efforts and virtues of Moslems in general and of Sufis in particular would be inexplicable without the eminent virtues of the Prophet; Islam itself would be inexplicable without them. We must nevertheless recognize that the traditional stories give only a general idea of these virtues with any certainty, and that in addition, they suggest to the Christian reader—even if he brings no ill will into play—an impression of unreality for which he cannot be blamed; and this by the inconsequences of these accounts as much as by their quite unnecessary hyperbolisms, objectively speaking.[9]

The desire to attribute to the Prophet, almost automatically and often to him alone, the height of all possible perfections, in many cases impedes the definition or description of real qualities. Thus, when it is said that the Prophet left behind him the two worlds with all their pleasures and that he was thus the greatest of ascetics—he to whom "women and perfumes" were made "lovable"—history gives us no element that corroborates this portrait, or which corroborates it with strength and precision, whereas it does show us with certainty that in the character of the Prophet there was no trace of pettiness.[10] If, on the contrary, we were told, on the basis of the principle of a nature sanctified in advance,[11] that the Prophet was *a*

9. Moreover one meets not only hyperbolisms as such, but also exaggerations in a reductive sense: for example, one exalts the "station" of a saint, and then one adds, in essence, that he never lied or stole, which is indeed the least of things; or one relates that a saint received in such and such a heavenly assembly such and such a sublime investiture, and then one adds that henceforth he had the duty of ensuring the strict observance of the religious prescriptions, which any cadi can do.

10. The contrary opinion proves, if not always prejudice or bad faith, at least a total lack of psychology or even simply of discernment, with regard to circumstances as well as with regard to men.

11. This is expressed by the "opening of the breast" of the infant

priori detached from things because he encountered through them their prefigurations *in divinis* — in which case the question of asceticism does not arise — we would have no difficulty in accepting such a proposition, given that we know that it is a question here of a possibility proper to the nature of the Messengers from Heaven.[12]

We have more than once had occasion to quote this formula of a Church Father: "God became man in order that man become God" — and to paraphrase it thus in Vedantic terms: "*Atmā* became *Māyā* in order that *Māyā* become *Atmā*"; or in Buddhist terms: "*Nirvāna* became *Samsāra* in order that *Samsāra* become *Nirvāna*." As regards the personality of the Prophet as an "avataric" phenomenon, we could say: the Logos became "average man"* in order that average man become the Logos; we offer this paraphrase as a key and in connection with what we said above, without its being necessary, we hope, to explain it in a detailed manner or to justify the terms used.

But let us return to the question of moral qualities: 'Asharī and others, in the name of the Islam of which they seek to be the spokesmen, demand a maximum of virtues on the basis of a minimum of metaphysical, or simply logical, intelligibility of God; in other words, they present an image of God which makes the effort to be virtuous as difficult as possible. In short, they replace logic by threats, even more then by enticement; which in the last analysis does wrong to both God and man.

Mohammed: two angels removed from his breast a clot of blood and replaced it with snow.

12. The Koran indicates this possibility in the words: "Verily thou art of a supereminent nature" *('alā khuluqin azīm)* (*Sura of the Pen,* 4); which forms a basis for appreciation, but not to the detriment of the other "Messengers" who, on the contrary, are included in this eulogy.

*The author has in mind the average man of a traditional civilization and not man diminished by the artificiality of the modern world. Traditional man has the sense of the sacred and has no triviality. (Translator's note)

According to the Asharite thesis, to which we have already referred, evil comes from God in the same way as good; God created men and made rules for them, but He was not obliged to do either one or the other; moreover, He can impose on men obligations which they are incapable of carrying out; He can punish a creature who has not sinned and without owing him any compensation; for He "doeth what He will," He owes nothing to man, He owes him no goodness, He has no obligation.[13] Still according to the same thesis, knowledge of God, which is incumbent upon man, results from Divine Law and not from intelligence. The same applies to the obedience which man owes to God: the intelligence is only there in order to draw the practical consequences from the divine commands. It seems to be forgotten that man, who not for nothing has the privilege of vertical stature and of speech, was created "in the image of God"; that God created him in order to have an interlocutor and not a slave limited to carrying out divine commands and to contravening them when God should so decide. This amounts to saying that 'Asharī confuses metaphysics with morality, or even with immorality in certain cases: he does not see that God having created man so as to have a "valid inter-

---

13. When the Koran says that "God doeth what He will," this means that the Principle, being infinite, possesses All-Possibility, from which spring forth the indefinitely diverse combinations of the particular possibilities. These possibilities are so to speak in constant battle with the impossible: if the color grey exists, it is to overcome — "as far as possible" precisely — the impossibility that black should be white or that white should be black; if there is a square whose sides are slightly convex, it is to overcome the impossibility — always "to the extent possible" — that a square should be round or a circle square. "With God all things are possible," said Christ; this means that the Divine Possible can always intervene "vertically" on planes whose possibilities are only "horizontal," or "natural," if one prefer.

locutor," "wishes to owe" something to man, otherwise He would not have created him;[14] and this is totally independent of the fact that man, as simple contingency, is nothing with regard to the Absolute, as is the whole world. In short Asharism denies that God is free to realize the possibility of a reciprocity between Himself and a creature; thus it is that it denies, always in the name of an ill-conceived divine freedom, the immanent logic of natural laws. What might be called the "ontological immorality" of 'Asharī arises from a religious anthropomorphism at grips with the baffling complexity of *Māyā*: It is attributing to one single Divine Subjectivity the divergent effects of the Divine Radiation; divergent effects, but perfectly compatible given that *Māyā* has its root in the principial order; whence a certain diversity in this order itself.[15] But perhaps, from the theological point of view, it was better to say in a monstrous fashion that God is the Master than not to say it at all, in a world in which everyone wants to be king.

In theological blunderings, there are grounds for scandal, but not more so in fact than in the formal divergences of the religions; not in the simple fact of their plu-

14. "Then We shall save Our Messengers and those who believe; thus it is incumbent upon Us (*haqqan 'alaynā* = "is a duty for Us") to save the believers," (*Sura of Jonah,* 103) and likewise: "And We took vengeance on those who sinned, and it is incumbent upon Us to succor the believers." (*Sura of the Romans,* 47). In other words, what is "incumbent" upon God, as a duty, is what is in His nature: He must succor the believers, not for the exclusive and accidental reason that He "wills it," but for the principial reason — actualized in specific circumstances — that by virtue of His nature He sustains the true and the good to which He will necessarily give final victory, being Himself Truth and Goodness. It is in the same sense that God "prescribed for Himself Mercy" (*Sura of Cattle,* 12 and 54); He is not merciful in His essence because He decides to be so, but He exercises Mercy because it is in His nature. He is not what He wills, but He wills what He is.

15. This is suggested, in Hebrew, by the plural *Elohim,* at least in a higher and "vertical" sense, the usual and "horizontal" sense doubtless referring to the Divine "Names."

rality—for one readily accepts the plurality of crystals or of flowers—but in the fact of their flagrant contradictions and their reciprocal anathemas. "And the light shineth in the darkness; and the darkness comprehended it not." These words, apart from their immediate sense, also apply to every Revelation insofar as it is not grasped in all its dimensions, we do not say by the few, but by the collectivity whose spokesmen are precisely the theologians. Religion is to a large extent in the hands of "psychics" and not "pneumatics"; the Word, in descending, adapts to the needs of "sinners" more than to those of the "righteous";[16] the collective soul collaborates in the outward face of the Revelation owing to the fact that it is the latter's plane of resonance.

*

*   *

But let us return to the pious excesses of language which seem to be authorized—or not prevented—by the point of view of faith. Ghazālī, who elsewhere criticizes the excesses of fear, relates in his *Ihyā*—rightly or wrongly —that Abū Bakr would have preferred to be a bird rather than a man, because of his fear of the Judgement; that Omar, for the same reason would have preferred to be a piece of straw; that Hasan al-Basrī would have considered himself lucky if he could receive the assurance that he would escape from hell after being there for a thousand years; that tens of thousands of people would have died of fright after having heard a sermon by David on hell; and

16. This results, in a Christian context, in exaggerations such as the following, which at least are not presented as esoterism: according to Pascal, "there are two classes of men, the saints who consider themselves guilty of every fault and the sinners who think they are guilty of nothing." One would like to know if the author of these words considered himself capable of every fault, and if not, why he attributed this sentiment to the saints; or inversely, since he attributed this sentiment to the saints, why he did not share it.

other stories of this kind. What can one conclude from these extravagances? Their demerit lies not only in the exaggeration in itself, but also in the isolation of the latter; this isolation is thought to make them more striking and more fully efficacious — one does not wish to adulterate the mystery of terror — but logically it makes them either all the more hopeless, or all the more improbable. Nonetheless, these shock-images manifest at one and the same time three values; the sense of the absolute, moral idealism, and indignation at the spectacle of worldly carelessness. They are nevertheless incompatible with gnosis, and incoherent when they refer to the state of soul of a saint; if this state of soul were ephemeral, one should say so right away. Let us recall that Al-Ghazālī was a Sufi and not one of the least, otherwise we would have no reason for drawing attention here to these things.

One may be surprised that in Islam the perspective of fear, which in its extremist formulations — when these are accepted at face value — removes practically all meaning from existence, is not opposed to marriage and in particular to polygamy, as if there were no logical and moral connection between fear and penance;[17] a connection which Moslems nevertheless understand very well when it comes to fasting. For Islam, only what diverts us from God, *de jure* or *de facto*, is contrary to fear; now the Sufis, while admitting that marriage may comprise this danger, envisage in the first place the sacred character of sexuality — its quality of Platonic remembrance in particular, which "causes us to desire paradise" — so that sexual en-

---

17. All the same it must not be forgotten that the numerous marriages of Hasan, the son of 'Alī had as their aim the creation of a caste of sharifs as large and diverse as possible. Nevertheless, and this is a completely different point: that a man who has four "legal" wives and several concubine slaves can be considered as "chaste" because he does not touch the hand of another woman, is for the Westerner one of the enigmas of the Moslem mentality; it is explained by a sort of habitual confusion of legalism and virtue.

joyment appears to them at least as being neutral with respect to fear of the Judgement, and as something that is related to trust and hope. Independently of this aspect of things, they look on conjugal life in a practical and social respect and thus with a view to procreation; finally, they see in it a means of escaping from the distracting preoccupation of the "goad of the flesh": sexual enjoyment being for them something spiritually neutral — and harmful only when it is sought after for itself, in which case it becomes "animal" and separates one from God[18] — they see no reason to expose themselves needlessly to the torment of the sexual instinct and to the distracting preoccupation which it involves. Some will object that this way of looking at things opens the door to every form of concupiscence, especially to the sin of gluttony, for if there is no limit to sexuality, there can be none to other satisfactions of the senses; this is false, for eating too much makes one ill, degrades one and makes one ugly, which is not the case as regards the conjugal life of healthy people, and in this inequality is the proof that the two items are not comparable, except, precisely, when they are both reduced to animality. Be that as it may, the Moslem "ascetic" *(zāhid)* flees the world, riches, ambitions, comfort, pleasures, food considered to be superfluous, even sleep, everything, save woman,[19] which does not prevent him from disparaging her on occasion; we put it in this way in order to

18. It should be noted that human animality is situated beneath animality as such, for animals innocently follow their immanent law and thereby enjoy a certain natural and indirect contemplation of the Divine Prototype; whereas there is decadence, corruption and subversion when man voluntarily reduces himself to his animality.

19. There are doubtless a few exceptions which "prove the rule." — Rūmī considers, with finesse and profundity and not without humor, that the sage is conquered by woman whereas the fool conquers her: for the latter is brutalized by his passion and does not know the *barakah* of love and delicate sentiments, whereas the sage sees in the lovable woman a ray from God, and in the feminine body an image of creative Power.

make the point that as an Arab dialectician he will say "women" and not "some women"—even though he might in fact be circumspect—so that logically he puts himself in the wrong even if he is right a thousand times over.

It goes without saying that a sexual mysticism, which by definition reveals the universality and immanence of Beatitude and so of Mercy, is incompatible with an accentuation of the fear of hell; now neither Islam in general nor Sufism in particular is founded on this perspective, but they necessarily permit its affirmation either incidentally or occasionally. At all events, if hell is a concrete and quasi-uncontrollable risk for the holiest of men—something that Islam does not teach but which certain extravagances seem to suggest, and which would drive all other men to despair—everyone would have to become a hermit, and there could be no question either of marrying or even of eating beyond the minimum that would prevent us from dying of hunger;[20] this is perhaps a truism, but in fact Sufi authors have not always been coherent in their manner of presenting—explicitly or implicitly—the compatibility between the fear of God and sexual life. For in short, the man who fiercely intends to renounce the world, and who "trembles and sweats" at the very thought of the Judgement cannot, in good logic, relax with his wives, as the Sunna permits or recommends; if he does so, he has no right to decry too much the world we live in, nor for that matter Paradise and the houris. Nor has he the right to proclaim in too shattering a manner that "God alone suffices him"—God alone in His exclusive transcendence—as if the creature did not by definition need the

20. This makes us think of a seeming divergence between St. John of the Cross and St. Theresa of Avila: having received a bunch of grapes, St. John considered that if one thought of the Justice of God, one could never eat them; whereas St. Theresa was of the opinion, that if one thought of the Mercy of God, one would always eat them.

gifts of God, and as if the Koran were not the first to affirm this.

Having spoken of fear, we must now say something of the point of view of confidence, which on the one hand complementarily compensates that of fear, and on the other hand nullifies the too-absolute expressions of the latter; moreover the legitimate point of view of fear likewise nullifies the possible excesses of the perspective of confidence. Confidence is neither levity nor temerity, any more than fear is dramatism or discouragement.

God created sinners so that He could forgive them, Ghazālī tells us: even though the quantity of our sins should stretch to heaven, God will forgive the believer who both hopes and asks for forgiveness; the idea of hell being the whip that chases believers towards Paradise. According to 'Alī, to despair of Mercy is, on the part of the sinner, a greater sin than all his other sins put together. But there is not only the argument of repentance, trust and Mercy, there is also that of the graces inherent in the sacramental formulas: above all the *Shadādah,* which effaces sins and leads to Paradise; then the formulas of praise which cause sins to be forgiven even though they be as "numerous as the waves on the ocean."[21] No doubt this perspective re-establishes equilibrium in the general doctrine, but it does not for all that abolish the excesses of the contrary perspective.[22]

In itself, there is no symmetry between Goodness and

21. One nevertheless insists on the importance of a mind turned towards the hereafter and detached from the here-below; this disposition being both condition and consequence.

22. Nor the logical incompatibility between the two theses. For if it is true that God created sinners to be able to forgive them and that despair of Mercy is a sin greater than all others combined, it cannot be equally true, that saints such as Abu Bakr and Omar were right in wishing to be a bird or a straw through fear of the divine Rigor. One and the same doctrine cannot bludgeon us with eschatological threats which objectively lead to despair, while ordering us to rejoice at the "licit" goods of this life.

71

Rigor, for the first is ontologically more real than the second; but in practice there is symmetry between them as regards the generality of pious men, and even asymmetry in favor of Rigor in relation to some men or to some aspect of human nature. Islam teaches nothing else, but it does so by means of an isolating dialectic, both accentuating and discontinuous, which seems characteristic of it as a result of a certain side of the Arab character.

As for the incoherence of Sufi morals, it is sometimes more apparent than real, for it can be the effect of an ellipsism that dissimulates particular intentions; Sufism indeed disposes of a casuistry in depth which is largely able to compensate, depending on the case, for the presence of a simplistic moralism, and which brings us back as if by stealth into an esoteric context.

*

* *

There is an attenuating circumstance in the case of excesses of the type "God suffices me" on the part of a polygamist — we do not need to return here to the compatibility in principle between ascesis and sexual life — and it is the following: one must take account of a difference of dimension between the spiritual intention, which pertains to principles, and life in the world and amongst creatures, which is of a contingent order. The ascetic *(zāhid)*, while he is in the *sacratum* of prayer or contemplation, may affirm a singleminded idealism that is independent of human concessions, contrivances and nuances, and he may later, outside this *sacratum*, live according to the laws of earthly life, without contradiction or hypocrisy; the effects of contemplation will by themselves regulate and adapt his behavior in the world, rather as a stone that falls into the water produces concentric circles. The too-absolute declarations of spiritual intention would be unrealistic and hypocritical if the contemplative were not aware of the *distinguo* that we have just explained, and if he took his

72

own words literally, something which, precisely, the Moslem *zāhid* does not and cannot do.

This brings us back to the question — which we have discussed in other writings — of the two spiritual subjectivities, one being that of the empirical individual, who cannot sincerely desire a "union" beyond Paradise, and the other, that of the spirit, which tends towards its own source and remains independent of every consideration of individual interest. *Advaita-vedānta* which has nothing individualistic and consequently nothing agitated about it, envisages only the second subjectivity and so to speak abandons the first to its fate, by placing it in the hands of the Divine Mother;[23] Sufism on the contrary accentuates the first subjectivity without for all that being unaware of the second, sometimes mixing the two in a way which gives rise to a dramatism akin to that of Christian mysticism. And this is all the more paradoxical in that there is in Islam itself a marked element of serenity, whose most general manifestation is resignation to the Will of *Allāh*, and which finds liturgical expression by this celestial mantle — divinely leveling — which is the call to prayer from the top of the minarets; now this omnipresent serenity is related to gnosis in that it derives fundamentally from the First Truth, and thus from the One which excludes all that is not It, and includes all that through It is possible.

*

* *

Let us return once more to the question of moralistic or ascetical extravagances: there is an attenuating circumstance, we have said, but not a total excuse. Doubtless the excess is accidental and not substantial; it is nonetheless blameworthy owing to the fact that the *zāhid* is not alone, he lives in a human society which, for its part, has a certain right to understand him, or at least not to be scandal-

23. For example, *Pārvatī, Lakshmi, Tripurasundarī, Shāradā, Sarasvatī.*

ized by him through no fault of its own; society would be at fault in this matter if its incomprehension were due to its lukewarmness or worldliness, which is not the case of the pious persons of whom we are thinking here. In spite of the prejudice of certain esoterists, the mistrust of the *'ulamā* — who have a right to exist as does the "letter" itself — is largely justified by the unintelligibility and the paradoxical nature of certain speculations or ascetico-mystical expressions.

In his "Chronicle of the Saints" *(Tadhkirat al-Awliyā)*, Attār relates the following incident: the serving-maid of the famous Rābi'ah Adawiyah was going to request an onion from a neighbor, but Rābi'ah forbade her, for she intended to ask for everything from God alone; she wanted to accept nothing from men. Whereupon a bird came and dropped an onion in the saint's saucepan; but the saint did not accept it, because, said she, it might come from the demon. The doubtful nature of this story already appears in the fact that it also circulates in an older and simpler version; but what interests us here is exclusively what is implied by the version which Attār has not hesitated to offer us. There are in fact two important remarks to make: firstly, it is not normal for man to ask God for what can or should be given to him by men; one does not have the right to expect supernatural aid for things which one normally obtains in a natural way. Secondly, one does not have the right to believe that a legitimate prayer can be answered by the demon, or that the demon can reply to our legitimate trust in God; otherwise God would have no reason to fulfill our prayers or to reward our trust, for He does not act to no purpose.[24] It will be said

24. The demon can answer an extravagant prayer which has no chance of being accepted by God, just as he can respond to an excessive and foolhardy trust; Rābi'ah could thus have been right to doubt the miracle, but in this case her doubt would amount to the condemnation of her prior attitude, which the hagiographer however had not dreamt of criticizing.

that the hagiographer was thinking only of virtues and symbolism; this is obvious, but it does not satisfy every logical need or every sense of proportion.

When, in "Sufis of Andalusia" *(Rūh al-Quds)*, we read that the hero, having received a luxurious house from the reigning prince,[25] gives it to the first beggar who arrives because he "has nothing else to give him," we are in the midst of absurdity, and this in several respects, namely with regard to the hero, the house, the prince, the beggar, and the Law; the intention of the story is clearly to indicate strongly—and perish all the rest—the disdain of things here-below and the sublimity of detachment and generosity. That conclusive facts envisaged in themselves, and logic practised without a moralizing hidden motive, can be guarantors of truth and serve the doctrinal or moral intention to be expressed, does not impress itself on the intention of our pious authors, who balk at envisaging a thing in itself, and thus "outside God"; thus one must read them with a patience which no doubt one owes to their excellent intentions and to their love of God and of sacred things.[26]

Very often Sufi authors, and religious authors in gen-

25. The hagiographer, who is here relating his own adventure, finds it appropriate to specify that the house cost 100,000 dirhams; and that in the 12th century.

26. In pointing out the weaknesses of certain categories of religious writings—and the religious character of Sufi writings is incontestable—some may reproach us with speaking of things of which the majority of Western readers are ignorant, and that in any event this is not the best way to prepare them for an understanding of Islam and Sufism. Our reply, on the one hand, is that there exists nowadays a rather considerable number of good translations of Islamic works and on the other hand, that we are addressing ourselves to readers with a certain knowledge of these works and who are allegedly interested in them; they have inevitably encountered—or will encounter—in the course of their reading, the pitfalls we have spoken of in this chapter. As for those readers who are in no wise troubled by these pitfalls—for "East is East and West is West"—it is obviously not for them that we are clearing the ground.

eral, give the impression of being just as much uninterested in the exactness of their facts as in the imperatives of logic, as if it were a question here of worldly matters; only the landmarks of morals, mystical life, theology seem to hold their attention, that is to say, they seek to make them as striking as possible and believe they cannot achieve this except at the expense of objective detail or even common sense. In their minds, the materiality of the facts seems to harm the expressivity of the symbol, whereas for the Westerner on the contrary this materiality supports the probability of the image and thus its instructive capacity; it is true that in this order of things, everything is a question of opportuneness and degree. No doubt one must admit in certain cases that the end justifies the means; this does not preclude that in other cases the means compromise the end, and this is what occurs, in our opinion, in the type of literature that we have in mind here. In this connection, it is necessary to point out above all the misuse of apologues and the habitual confusion between the real and the imaginary, born of a tendency to exaggeration.[27]

We could adduce in this context the fact that the Aryan, insofar as he is observer and philosopher, has a tendency to describe things as they are, while the Semite, who is a moralist, readily presents them as they ought to be according to his pious sentiment; he transcends them by sublimizing them before having had time to extract from them the arguments comprised in their nature. This tendency obviously does not prevent him from being a philosopher when he wants to be, but we are speaking here of the most immediate and most general predispositions; the abuse of apologues and of quantitative images incontestably bears witness to this, especially in the case of the Arabs, although such excesses can be found in every religious climate, the same psychological causes

27. Ibn Al-Jawzī, in the 12th century, criticizes these extravagances in his *Kitāb al-Qussās*.

readily giving rise to the same effects.[28]

We have just confronted Oriental worship of the "symbol" with Western worship of the "fact"; now if the first can give rise to abuses, it is only too obvious—and history proves it abundantly—that the same is true, and *a fortiori*, of the second tendency, and this applies not only in the scientific domain, and in the wake of Aristotle, but even on the religious plane. From the beginning Catholics have had fits of "pious skepticism," which they confuse with realism, and this occurs in private spirituality as well as in theology;[29] this intermittent temptation has permit-

28. Buddhists in particular do not deny themselves pious exaggeration, at least in some aspects or sectors of the *Mahāyāna*.

29. There is something of this in Thérèse de Lisieux—despite her angelic nature—when she diminishes the Blessed Virgin in order to bring her "nearer": whereas hagiographic tradition takes account of what is implied by the unheard of privilege of the "Immaculate Conception" and of divine Maternity, Thérèse was unable to reconcile the majesty and the exceptional graces with simplicity and goodness; when tradition says that Mary, at the age of three, went to the Temple with a heart "burning with love for God," Thérèse considers it more probable—because more banal—that the Virgin went there "simply to obey her parents"; likewise the life of the Virgin at Nazareth, according to the same sentiment, had to be "completely ordinary," as presented by the Gospel, so it is said (*Novissima Verba*, collected by Mother Agnes of Jesus); now apart from the fact that the Gospel says nothing about the daily life of Mary, the life of a co-redeeming *Mater Dei* could not in any event be "ordinary" in the stupidly conventional sense of the word. For Thérèse, the Blessed Virgin is "mother" more than "queen," as if Mary were not great and mysterious before making herself little and intimate; and it is for the queen, not her subjects, to decide when and how she intends to be mother, the worth and the charm of the maternal intimacy residing here precisely in its combination with majesty. Moreover, if one thinks one has to attribute to the Bessed Virgin, in order to be able to "imitate" her and love her in a more inane manner, a sort of bourgeois smallness devoid of extraordinary gifts which would oblige us to too much admiration—this is what Thérèse intends—one ought also to claim the same reassuring mediocrity for Christ, in whom, however, one cannot deny the most supereminent human gifts; now what is absurd for the Son is equally so for the Mother, for analogous reasons.

ted the growing infiltration of the profane spirit, right up to the triumph of modernism and so of the "world" and of "man," all this with the help of the creative and innovating mania of the Europeans, in regard to which the Biblical stability and holy monotony of Islam play the role of divine warnings. Islam has been accused of "sterilizing" a whole section of humanity, of having "arrested" history; it is one of the most useful things it could do.

*

* *

Some might take the view that the theological or philosophical framework of an idea that is both true and fundamental — such as ontological monism *(wahdat al-wujūd)* — is of little importance, even if this framework leaves much to be desired; it is true that in Islam — inasmuch as it is a world of dogma and faith — the thing that is important is "what" one explains and not "how" one explains it. For the "what" is divine, thus absolute, whereas the "how" is human, thus contingent and provisional; here lies the whole opposition between faith and reasoning, or between Revelation and thinking. Seen from this angle, weak or even aberrant explanations of indisputable truths represent nothing other than apologetic intentions in the interest of faith; it is not these that count, it is the idea that they are supposed to make accessible; that which serves the truth is true, according to this "intellectual morality."

In conformity with the tendencies of Islamic piety in particular and with the Semitic monotheistic perspective in general, the Moslem — apart from those Hellenized by vocation — does not seek to be a "philosopher," that is to say a man who "doubts" and who thinks "outside God," outside faith and grace; he expects therefore everything from inspiration; he has no wish to be a Prometheus. Thus it happens that an almost stereotypical zeal takes precedence over logic, the latter being the *ancilla theologiae*; whence there sometimes arises an exorbitant desire to extract from absurdity the elixer of truth that is vehicled by a right intention nourished by the treasures of Revelation.[30]

Quite fortunately one is not faced solely with the alternative between a credulous and undisciplined language of "faith" and a skeptical and pedantic language of "reason"; or between a language that is absurd but efficacious, and another that is logical but inoperative.[31] It is nevertheless between these two poles or these two excesses that the human mind seems to vacillate, something for which neither a healthy faith, which is lucid, nor a healthy intellection, which is pious, is directly responsible.[32]

In a completely different category from the overflowing imagery of an unbridled fideism are the phenomena — described in mystical books — pertaining to what we could call objectivizing symbolist inspiration, which is drawn from the archetypes of the collective religious psychism and thanks to which spiritual intuitions assume objective and sensible forms; in other words, inward contacts with heavenly realities become outward experiences, by the effect of a mechanism proper to every religious cosmos, and comparable to individual imagination, although operating in the physical world by projecting into it symbolic phenomena.[33] For this there is both an objective and a subjective condition: the first is a very powerful subtle aura which envelops and nourishes a religious world, at

30. We have dealt with all these questions — with certain accentuations which we shall not repeat here — in our book *Logic and Transcendence*, in the chapter "Oriental Dialectic and its Roots in Faith."

31. The West, nourished on philosophy, had need of the language of faith, which Christianity provided; but Christianity in turn had need of the language of reason, which was provided by scholasticism.

32. "Lucid" by virtue of a sense of orthodoxy; "pious" by virtue of a sense of the sacred.

33. Of an analogous order are, in the visions of Anne Catherine Emmerich, the purely symbolical images which are interspersed with historically adequate facts.

least for as long as it is sufficiently homogeneous; the second is an appropriate receptivity on the part of men—a certain naïvety, quite capable nevertheless of the "discernment of spirits"—incompatible with the enfeeblement and "congelation" of a world that has become impious. The order of phenomena which we have in mind here does not, properly speaking, pertain to the miraculous since the celestial intervention therein is only indirect; nor is it a question of personal fantasies since the phenomena are outward although their forms are determined, precisely, by the style of the collective religious psychism. It is thus that one can explain the rain of somewhat gratuitous, but not legendary, marvels which occurred during periods of great mystical fervor and within unfissured religious worlds; the partition between the material and the subtle is blurred, the psychic is objectivized; we might also say that the psycho-spiritual is exteriorized to the extent that the believing mentality is interiorized.

*

* *

Compared with the case of the fideists or inspirationists with their lack of concern for coherence, the case of the Greek sophists and scientists and their successors presents exactly the opposite excess: logic on the one hand and phenomena on the other are self-sufficient and they are therefore used as if they were cut off from their roots; whence the philosophical, scientific and cultural monstrosities which made, and which make, the modern world. And since, in every work, the essential content, or reason for existence, takes precedence over expression and accident, we must obviously prefer the aberrant expression of the truth to a dialectic that is brilliant but made aberrant through its content; one would like to apologize for having to mention all of this.

That is to say, and we are not afraid of repeating ourselves in recalling the following: just as in the case of profane thinkers one may find perfectly formulated reasonings, so, inversely, the writings of a given gnostic may contain intellections that are badly expressed, and even compromised by weak reasonings, whose function nevertheless, is to act as their support; now one owes it to the underlying truth, to the very extent that it is lofty and decisive, to discern it even if in its contingent formulation there are elements of error which disfigure it without for all that rendering it unusable, rather as one owes to one's parents a favorable prejudice even when they err through excess of zeal.

The perfect man, wrote a certain Sufi — and we spoke of this at the beginning of the present chapter — is one who is extinguished before the world to the point of no longer seeing anything but God; or one who only sees God to the point of no longer seeing the world. This Sufi did not realize this, for on the one hand, it is not realizable and on the other hand, for this very reason it does not have to be realized; this ideal nevertheless bears witness to a heroic intensity towards the Divine, and this is what counts here; and it may even be that the Sufi did not seek to say anything else, which brings us back to the problem of Oriental ellipsism.[34] Be that as it may, some might still object that the vision of the Principle alone is perfectly within the scope of the "pneumatic"; no doubt, but it does not exclude the simultaneous vision of objects — as is proved by the life of any Sufi or *jīvan-mukta*, not to mention the Prophets and the *Avatāras* — just as the realization of the "Self" does not exclude an individuality liberated from concupiscence.[35]

34. Which consists, as we have said more than once, in isolating an idea from its often necessary context, and then in overemphasizing it to the point of giving it a quasi-absolute character; and to the point of ruining, logically speaking, the idea in question, whose overall intention is nevertheless plausible.

35. This is shown irrefutably by the theological expression — applied to Christ — of "true man and true God."

In a completely general manner, it must be fully understood that we are not criticizing the incomprehensibility of many Sufi texts, something that is inevitable in the absence of commentaries that provide the keys to this particular language; we would not dream of reproaching a Hallāj or a Niffarī for the obscureness of their expressions, any more than we would dream of reproaching the Song of Songs for such an obscureness. It suffices us *a priori*, in the absence of keys, to perceive the beauty, the grandeur, the profundity, the power of the language, its perfume of truth and majesty, quite apart from the fact that the incomprehensibility cannot be total and that, moreover, there are keys which end by delivering their secrets, depending on their nature and on our receptivity. That keys of this kind should sometimes be combined with the weaknesses of which we have spoken, is a completely different matter, which does not concern the keys in themselves or those who use them correctly and with the best of rights.

*

*   *

We believe we have alluded more than once to the mistrust shown by the fideists towards rational investigation in matters of faith; a classic example of this is Hanbalite fideism, which is refractory to all symbolist interpretation of Koranic images, even to the point of absurdity. According to this school, we must accept Koranic images that express a quality or attitude of God "without asking how," thus without transposition, even in cases where the meaning results from the image itself, for example when it is said that God is "Light," or that He is "seated" on a "Throne" or when the text speaks of the "Hand" of God. The fideists will say that it is the Koranic word itself which coincides *ipso facto* with its interpretation *(ta'wīl)* and which thus implicitly constitutes it, so that all explanation of the image becomes superfluous; we would reply that in this case the very notion of *ta'wīl* loses all its meaning and that in reality the symbol-word suggests its intention by its very nature, the sufficient reason of the metaphor being precisely its capacity to transmit a meaning that is superimposed on the raw image, and to transmit it without any possible doubt.[36] This is not to say that the fideistic point of view has no legitimacy in itself; it can be applied perfectly in cases where the image is mysterious and requires to be assimilated in an almost eucharistic manner, but not when the image has no sense outside of its obviously metaphorical meaning.[37]

That Ibn 'Arabī should occasionally sustain the abusive fideism of the Hanbalites is all the more paradoxical in that he himself practices the most audacious interpretation,[38] which seems to consist in reducing every Koranic verse to a statement more or less directly concerning either the Divine Essence or Supreme Love, contrary not only to the immediate sense of the text, but to the very detriment of its coherence and its obvious intention; one can be justifiably astonished at a procedure as unneces-

36. Consequently, to say with the motazelites that the "Throne" is the authority or the power of God, is not even *ta'wīl*, it is simply semantics and good sense. One knows the incident in which Ibn Taimiyah came down one step of the pulpit *(minbar)* in order to show that "this is how God comes down"; we would say that if these fideists have no wish to use their intelligence, at least they should not forbid others to do so. And since the Arabs make wide use of metaphors, why should God not do so when He speaks to them, especially since He does so in their own language *(lisānun 'arabīyun mubīn)*.

37. Ibn Hanbal undoubtedly had a valid presentiment when he excluded, along with speculative thought, aberrant thought, for it is better to limit oneself to believing that God created the world "from nothing" than to end up with heresies as a result of asking how He did it.

38. According to a theological opinion, explicative truth is only valid if it comes from inspiration and not from reflection; this opinion is either false — since truth is always truth — or else true, but in this case the notion of inspiration includes that of intellection or fuses with it.

sary as it is paradoxical, given that truth has other resources, to say the least. One of the keys to this enigma seems to be the idea that Revelation above all provides words and that it is incumbent on sages to explain them, if necessary by meticulously seeking the most far-fetched etymology, and at the risk of contradicting the literal meaning, or of contradicting it at least on the esoteric, or so-called esoteric, level; it seems to us obvious, on the contrary, that Revelation above all presents ideas, and not isolated words or images cut off from their necessary context, and that this is the very reason for the existence of the divine discourse. These ideas admittedly give rise to a variety of interpretations, but they nevertheless do not authorize us to isolate each detail by sublimizing it out of its context, to the detriment of logic and coherence, and especially to the detriment of the very intentions of the discourse.

Tafsīr, "explanation," is the "outward" *(zāhir)*, semantic, historical and theological exegesis of the Koran; *ta'wīl*, "interpretation,"[39] is its "inward" *(bātin)*, symbolist, moral, mystical, mythological, metaphysical commentary. According to the Koran, "no one knows its interpretation but God." This means that man can only know it by divine inspiration, and not by reasoning alone—but inspiration and reason are not mutually exclusive since the one can produce or actualize the other. This also opens the door to an inspirationism that is often problematical because contemptuous of intelligence. *Ta'wīl* comprises degrees: for example, when the Koran rejects idol worship, idols may mean, in addition to the literal sense, things to which we are unduly attached, or these attachments themselves; but they can also mean, more profoundly, forms as such, including the constituent elements of religion and religion itself, and then we are in

---

39. Literally: "to return to the origin," that is, to proceed from form to essence.

the midst of esoterism, not of the "prolonging" but of the "transcending" kind, and thus secret by its paradoxical and explosive nature. This is no doubt the source of the opinion — unacceptable, in our view — that a word or a phrase may "esoterically" have a meaning contrary to the one that it has in itself; or that this meaning may assert itself when the word or phrase is applied to the Divine Nature, on the basis that every Koranic expression must have a meaning that applies to God and the love of God, this meaning being positive as a result of the application in question.[40]

*

* *

Another matter, in this context of semi-esoterism, is the frequent disproportion between means and end. That is to say, there are ascetical and disciplinary measures which have no meaning except for passional men, given to ambition and vanity, not to say pride, and consequently disqualified for gnosis; now it is precisely with a view to gnosis that a certain "esoterism" imposes these measures on men who are qualified and thus who have no need of them, as well as on men who have need of them, and who

40. An example of an interpretation that is inadequate through inadvertence is the assertion that the Koranic prohibition of idol worship means "esoterically" that the *faqīr* should only obey God, which is absurd from the human or social point of view, as well as from the spiritual point of view; in fact, this idea has nothing to do with idolatry, for the idolator cannot "obey" an idol, which the Koran reproaches precisely for being deaf and dumb; and the man who obeys necessarily does so with regard to a being endowed with consciousness, not an "idol." — Ghazālī, who was far from being hostile to Sufism, criticized the extravagances *(tāmmāt)* of certain Sufis; according to him, it is forbidden and harmful to divert sacred words or formulations from their obvious meaning, for, as he says, this ruins one's confidence in the actual wording of the divine text. This is the condemnation, without appeal, of the exegesis of Ibn 'Arabī, as well as of a certain Shi'ite exegesis.

by this very fact, are not qualified.[41] In saying this, we are
not losing sight of the fact that there is not only profane
man but also man insofar as he carries in his soul the
temptation to profanity, which requires or allows of disciplinary measures; but these measures, precisely, must be
proportioned to the substance of the individual, even admitting that there is here no rigorous line of demarcation.

A Westerner desirous of following an esoteric way
would find it logical first of all to inform himself of the
doctrine, then to enquire about the method and finally
about its general conditions; but the Moslem of esoteric
inclination—and the attitude of the Kabbalist is doubtless
analogous—has definitely the opposite tendency: if one
speaks to him of metaphysics, he will find it natural to reply that one must begin at the beginning, namely with
pious exercises and all sorts of religious observances;
metaphysics will be for later. He does not seem to realize
that in the eyes of the Westerner, as also of the Hindu,[42]
this is to deprive the pious practices of their sufficient reason—not in themselves of course but with a view to
knowledge—and to make the way almost unintelligible;
and above all, the Semitic zealot does not see that understanding of doctrine cannot result from a moral and individualistic zeal, but that on the contrary it is there to in-
augurate a new dimension and to elucidate its nature and
purpose. The moralistic attitude moreover is only blameworthy through its ignorance of the opposite point of view
or through its exaggeration, for in fact, the doctrine deserves on our part an element of reverential fear; even our

41. The Imām Abu 'l-Hasan ash-Shādhilī is one of the Sufis who
very clearly saw this contradiction and avoided it in their method; he
saw nothing objectionable in his disciples practicing lucrative profes-
sions and wearing elegant clothes, and did not dream of sending pa-
tricians to beg in front of mosques.

42. And thus of the Aryan in general, except for groups totally
Semiticized by Islam. Christianity only Semiticized Europe partially
and in certain respects.

own spirit does not belong to us, and we only have full access to it to the extent that we know this. If it is true that doctrine explains the meaning of devotion, it is equally true that devotion has a certain right to precede doctrine, and that doctrine deserves this.

As regards lower moral disciplines presented as stages towards higher intellectual and spiritual results, the great question that arises is knowing whether or not metaphysical ideas act on the will of such and such a man, or whether on the contrary they remain inoperative abstractions; that is to say whether or not they unleash interiorizing and ascending acts of the will and affective dispositions of the same order. If this is the case, there is no need to seek to create a distaste in the person in question for a world which already hardly attracts him, or for an ego which already has no more illusions or ambitions, at least not at the level that would justify crude disciplines; it is pointless to impose on the "pneumatic" attitudes which for him are meaningless and which, instead of humbling him in salutary fashion, can only bore and distract him. To think otherwise — but there are here many degrees to consider — is to place oneself outside esoterism and sapience, whatever be the theories to which one thinks one can or must refer; it is to forget in particular that the "pneumatic" is the man in whom the sense of the sacred takes precedence over other tendencies, whereas in the case of the "psychic" it is the attraction of the world and the accentuation of the ego that take priority, without mentioning the "hylic" or "somatic" who sees in sensory pleasures an end in itself. It is not a particularly high degree of intelligence that constitutes initiatic qualification, it is the sense of the sacred — or the degree of this sense — with all the moral and intellectual consequences that it implies. The sense of the sacred separates from the world and at the same time transfigures it.

Whoever contemplates the Divine Majesty assimilates something of the latter, and he does so in parallel with a consciousness of his own nothingness; this results more-over from the fact that, according to a famous *hadīth*, God becomes "the eye with which he (the contemplative) sees and the hand with which he acts," and so in the last analy-sis the heart through which he is. This amounts to saying that the sense of the sacred, in spite of its relationship with fear, does not imply servility, any more than the sense of truth implies narrowness; esoterism is neither petty nor fanatical. "The soul is all that it knows," as Aristotle said, and the highest function of man is the knowledge of God, which gives its imprint to everything that is legitimately human.

Conception, meditation, concentration, conforma-tion; that is to say: concept of Unity with its intrinsic and extrinsic mysteries;[43] assimilating meditation, and uni-tive concentration, on Unity and its mysteries; moral con-formation to Unity, to its mysteries and its demands; these, together with the appropriate traditional supports, are the constituent elements of the Way. Moral confor-mation, we said: every spirituality indeed demands the intrinsic virtues as well as discipline in outward behavior and possibly a particular purgative ascesis; this derives from the intelligence as well as from the principle that "God is beautiful and loves beauty" *(hadīth)*; but it has no connection with ambition and perfectionism, in short with attitudes which, precisely, are lacking in beauty as well as in intelligence.

*

* *

Philosophy is one thing, the Sufis say, and inspiration is another; the first comes from men and the second from God. In theory, that is completely clear; but in practice, what is the significance of the fact that a certain Sufi claims for a certain book an inspiration coming either from God or from the Prophet?

43. Absoluteness, Infinitude, Perfection, Transcendence, Im-

Firstly, there can be no question of attributing to mystical books the degree of inspiration of the Koran or the Veda; but it is possible that they are situated at the secondary degree of inspiration, the one the Hindus designate by the term *smriti* and which is that of the *Purānas*, and there are still several other levels to be considered, whose significance is increasingly relative. Relativity of inspiration is connected with the mystery referred to in the following saying, which is perhaps a *hadīth*: "The divergence of the learned (of God) is a blessing." This mystery also includes, at the highest level, the divinely foreseen divergences of the religions, but here relativity has another meaning and another import. The Divine Inspirer—or the "angel of inspiration" *(malak al-ilhām)*—on becoming subjectivized gives rise to many refractions: "water takes on the color of the vessel," as Junayd said; even the great revelations have to take account of the resources of a collective mentality, and they cannot avoid suffering some damage through "shining in the darkness." However paradoxical that may seem, an intrinsically absolute conviction can have an extrinsically relative significance, but in this case there is obviously a different relationship; "no one cometh unto the Father but by me," Christ said on the basis of an inward absolute truth, which nevertheless does not prevent other religions from being valid in their turn, independently of Christ, but on the basis of the same truth, insofar as it is essential and thereby universal, and not insofar as it assumes in the case of Christ, a particular extrinsic significance personified precisely by Jesus.

Hallāj claimed, for a few lines written by his hand, an inspiration "equal to that of the Koran," and this is why Junayd did not hesitate to curse him; a certain number of Sufis blamed or condemned Hallāj for his *Ana 'l-Haqq* ("I am the Truth" = God), and yet tradition finally accepted

manance; then the prefigurations of the cosmos in the Principle on the one hand, and the projections of the Principle in the cosmos on the other.

both Hallāj and Junayd and the Sufis in question. The fact that Ibn 'Arabī wrote under heavenly inspiration does not bind Islamic orthodoxy, it does not even bind Sufi orthodoxy, as is proved by the negative attitude of the Mawlawiyah with regard to the *Shaykh al-Akbar*; and this is all the more plausible in that Sufism does not recognize any absolute authority in matters of metaphysics, whereas Vedantism recognizes itself in Gaudapāda, in Govinda and in Shankarāchārya. The undisputed authorities of Sufism — those of the first centuries — refer only to the ascetical and mystical method, and not to a sapiential doctrine properly so-called.

*

* *

If we note, with great reluctance, the lack of critical sense and other misdeeds of sentimentalism in many religious books whose level ought to exclude such weaknesses, it must be understood that we do not include in the notion of "sentimentalism" either the sense of beauty or love in itself, any more than we include in it contempt for things that are contemptible; sentimentalism consists, not in having sentiments, but in falsifying the truth as a result of them. To be a sentimentalist does not consist in knowing that two and two make four and at the same time loving something that deserves to be loved, it consists in persuading oneself that two and two make three or five simply because one desires to praise extravagantly something that one loves, rightly or wrongly; because one feels able in this way to corroborate or serve some idea that one is fond of, or because one thinks that such and such a truth demands by way of consequence such and such an excess, be it positive or negative. In short it consists in introducing a quantitative and dynamic element — and one that favors thoughtlessness — into the domain of the qualitative and the static, and in not knowing that truth is beautiful by itself and not by our zeal; and inversely, that our zeal

90

is only beautiful when it flows from truth.

A plausible explanation of the incoherence that one encounters in many Sufi writings is, in certain cases, the fact that the authors write when they are in a spiritual "state" *(hāl)*, and because they are in it; we have referred to this above. These states have empirically something absolute about them; consequently a given state presents itself as being unconnected with another and equally possible state. Now the authors see in these states sources of inspiration, and of course not without reason; they do not dream of re-reading what they have written, nor, least of all, of submitting their productions to the scrutiny of a critical intelligence which in their eyes is "profane" because not ecstatic, and thus alien to the breath of the Spirit; they leave to the reader the task of fishing for pearls in the deepest and darkest of waters. "Do not approach prayer when you are intoxicated," the Koran nevertheless says, and this order has many meanings, depending on levels and analogies.[44]

Islam as a whole has escaped that formidable pitfall, the abuse of intelligence—which neither ancient Greece nor the modern West has escaped—and this has enabled it to perpetuate the world of the Bible; but it has not escaped the opposite pitfall, which we have sufficiently described in the course of this book and which may be said to be the ransom, for the victory over luciferism, of the intelligence. According to an artificial dilemma, but one that is psychologically real for the Semitico-Western mentality, there is an antinomy between science and faith: the man who believes does not think, and the man who thinks does not believe; Islam is not unaware of this dilemma,

---

44. It has been asserted that Ibn 'Arabī wrote in a state of ecstatic inspiration, and that in this state he disdained the laws of logic; now it is necessary to distinguish between inspiration properly so-called, which is objective and which has nothing to do with ecstasy, and a subjective inspiration which on the contrary is derived from it, but which it would be wrong, in fact, to assimilate to inspiration in the or-

but in its case faith curbed the insatiable curiosity of science.

In an ardently religious climate in which faith is all and in which thought, considered as conjectural by definition, is more or less nothing, one must expect the logic of lovers: everything good — however absurd — that one says of God, the Prophet, sacred things, is true, as if truth were guaranteed by the sublimity of the object; to reflect is then almost a sin, since thinking appears like the manifestation of doubt and of unhealthy, or even luciferian, curiosity. This is the point of view of *bhakti* which is unaware, either through inexperience or by principle, of the humble serenity of pure intellection; humble because impersonal, and serene because it conforms to That which is. All this doubtless seems like an over-simplification, but one sometimes has to choose between the risk of simplifying things and the risk of not being able to say anything at all; schematic *distinguos* exist, they have their reason for existence and they by no means exclude implicit compensations or nuances, any more than the distant view of a landscape, necessary for revealing its main features, excludes the details that one observes when travelling through it.

It is important not to lose sight of the fact that the fideistic and dialectical "naïvety"[45] that we are referring to here remains completely independent of the eminent lucidity of the Arabs in matters of law, philosophy, science, art and politics; in short, independent of everything that

dinary sense of the term. One may in any case ask oneself if it is legitimate and useful to write in a state of "drunkenness," unless it be a case of texts whose reason for existence is to give expression to such a state.

45. Fideistic: to believe what one considers one has to believe under the cover of dogmatic data, without asking whether this will convince or "hold water"; dialectical: to deal with a particular point by isolating it and intensifying it, without asking whether this is suitable in itself, and compatible with what one previously said, or with other points that are just as valid.

constituted the prestige of their civilization during the whole of the Middle Ages.[46] The fact is that in the Arab soul, which can fall from the most obstinate incredulity into the most simplistic credulity, an acute rationality opposes an overflowing enthusiasm, either chivalric and erotic, or religious and mystical, and this dilemma gives rise to opposite crystallizations as well as to diverse combinations.

When we speak of the "Arab soul," we are not unaware that it was relatively diverse from pre-Islamic times in the sense that religious indifferentism was characteristic of the Arabs of the Center and the North, whereas those of the South were distinguished by a rather contemplative temperament; but they were homogeneous as regards their qualities of nobility. The "Arab miracle"—the lightning-like expansion of Islam and the glories of medieval Islamic civilization—presupposes and includes a spirit of magnanimity whose roots are plunged in the pre-Islamic Bedouin mentality, and which—whatever the falsifiers of history may say—contributed to the almost unprecedented phenomenon of the tolerance of the Moslem conquerors of the early centuries, hence when the Arab influence was predominant in Islam. Bedouin magnanimity consisted essentially in "virility" *(murūwah)*—in the sense of the Latin word *virtus*—and in "chivalry" *(futuwwah),* which comprised above all courage, generosity and hospitality; the most precious, the most fragile and the most specifically Arab feature—in the context of the Middle East—being the virtue of generosity.

In a completely general sense, and independently of any racial or ethnic question, it must be said that there are gifts that exclude one another, not indeed in principle or in privileged cases, but in the majority of those who en-

46. Inversely, the critical logicism of the Europeans—but everything is relative—by no means precludes passional ideologies, be these philosophical or political, and these are obviously more harmful than the flagrant and ingenuous contradictions of a hasty fideism.

joy one kind or another; it seems to be thus in the case of mystical intuition and reasoning. To take note of this, we must insist, does not mean that one considers it to be a necessity, but the *de facto* incompatibility — which obviously comprises many gradations — is a fact that one is well and truly obliged to keep in mind, whatever be the explanation one seeks to give to it.

But there is also in this order of ideas another point to consider and which is crucial: the key to many enigmas in the realm of spiritual thought is the fact that God requires of men that they be pious and virtuous, and not that they be intelligent; this provides the justification for a pious unintelligence, but is unconnected with gnosis and esoterism. Obviously God forbids men to make a bad use of their intelligence — persistent error being moreover in the will rather than in the mind — but He cannot blame them for not possessing an intelligence which was not given to them. That unintelligence can set up house with piety, that it can even, accidentally and sporadically, enter the realm of what should be wisdom, one is forced to admit, although in certain cases one hesitates to do so for fear of being disrespectful or ungracious; moreover, one all too often forgets the blinding evidence that it is better to follow truth stupidly than to follow error intelligently, all the more so as truth in any case neutralizes unintelligence at least to a certain extent, whereas on the contrary error can only pervert and corrupt the mind. In a word, the world of passions is necessarily also that of stupidity — intelligence solidary with this world itself becoming stupidity — so that religion, condemned to being put in the same boat with it, cannot avoid a few venial sins, which, if not of course "against the spirit," are at least against intelligence.

Contrary to a certain sentimental prejudice, the Holy Spirit does not have the function of making good a lack of intelligence or of abolishing stupidity; it can make it inoffensive or limit the harm it may cause; it can also reduce it to silence, which it does above all by humility. The miracle of humility is precisely that it alone is able to transmute unintelligence into intelligence, as far as this is possible; the humble man is intelligent by his very humility.

God requires from each man what each man can and must give; but from the intelligent man he requires in addition intelligence in the service of truth, for which it is made and through which it lives.[47] In some people, moreover, intelligence resides less in their theology than in their sanctity; nonetheless the spiritual norm lies in an equilibrium between thought and virtue, between mind and beauty.

Intelligence is only beautiful when it does not destroy faith, and faith is only beautiful when it is not opposed to intelligence.

47. One will recall here the parable of the talents, which refers to all possible gifts and to the duties that derive from them.

CHAPTER 4

Human Premises of a Religious Dilemma

If one strives too much to make transcendent truths accessible, one runs the risk of betraying them; if one strives too much not to betray them, one runs the risk of not making them accessible. This dilemma, which already exists at the level of the general religion, occurs to an even greater degree at the level of esoterism.

When one speaks of accessibility, it is obvious that one is referring implicitly to an understanding concerning this accessibility; now human mentalities are diverse and give rise to several degrees of receptivity. It is of this diversity or inequality that the caste system in Hinduism takes account, at least in respect of spirituality; admittedly, social· functions are not independent of spirituality, but it is not the social aspects of caste that concern us here. The advantage of the Hindu system is that it greatly favors the purity of esoteric spirituality; in the absence of such a system, esoterism becomes too closely linked with the average collective mentality which cannot be proportionate to the demands of a disinterested perspective or, in other words, cannot be entirely free from denominational narcissism.

Islam, like Christianity, is not exclusively addressed to the higher human categories, and this goes without saying, since it is a question of religions; moreover, it does not envisage "contemplatives" separately from "actives," or "hylics" separately from "psychics," which amounts to saying that in practice it puts *kshatriyas* of con-

97

templative tendency in the place of *brāhmanas*, and *vaishyas* of hylic tendency in the place of *shūdras*.[1] This being so, Moslems accentuate, in their language and psychology, the *vaishya* element more than the *kshatriya* element, because the *vaishya* is the average, practical, reasonable, and balanced man; his way, quite naturally, is *karma-mārga*, the way of works and merit, thus also of fear, and this is why the language and the general climate of Sufism — which nevertheless is "brahmanical" or "pneumatic" by its nature — are paradoxically molded by the mentality of the *vaishya* and the way of *karma*, even though, within this framework, they combine with the *kshatriya* spirit,[2] hence with an element of combativeness and of *bhakti*. From this amalgam there results a language which is both sagely moralizing and harshly perfectionistic which, to say the least, is anything but congenial to disinterested contemplativity; but it is also necessary to say that it is precisely the combination of the prudent realism of the merchant with the generous and intrepid idealism of the warrior which, in the Islamic perspective, is taken to represent synthetic and therefore final perfection;[3] but this, whatever be the reasons of Providence, has no connection with

1. Let us recall that the *brāhmana* represents the contemplative and sacerdotal mentality, the *kshatriya*, the active, combative, dynamic, noble, heroic mentality; the *vaishya*, the mercantile or artisanal mentality — or again that of the peasant according to the case, the *vaishya* mentality being "horizontal" in a certain sense. As for the *shūdra*, he is a materialist by his nature; his virtue is obedience.

2. The idea that man can attain to knowledge *(jnāna)* through action *(karma)* — an idea that the Vedantists reject — is fairly common in average Sufism, knowledge being in practice confused, in this case, with salvation pure and simple.

3. The mentality of 'Ashari and even of Ghazāli was basically that of a chivalrous merchant; this was the mentality of the Arabs, and the other peoples of the Near East were at least predisposed to it. "The essential of the Moslem city is the market" as Massignon said: one might also say — and Ibn Khaldūn saw this — that in Islam the merchant element is represented especially by the sedentaries, and the warrior element *a priori* by the nomads.

esoterism and the demands that gnosis makes in principle.

The element "intellection" or "contemplation" is affirmed, in Islam, by the dogma of unity and by the metaphysics that pertains to it, and psychologically by the accentuation of the elements "certainty" and "serenity." The element "combativeness," for its part, is affirmed by the holy war and its spiritual applications, and fundamentally by the Bedouin qualities of nobility and generosity; this chivalrous "verticality" most often provides the framework for contemplative heroism, as is shown by the interiorization of the holy war. As for the "horizontal" element, of which the merchant is probably the most readily graspable representative, this determines, as we have alluded above, the general or average style of theology and piety; this mentality is dry, prudent and practical, it is closer to respectability than to greatness; it has in any case the advantage of stability, as does indeed the sacerdotal mentality, but with the heaviness proper to "horizontality."[4] The "hylic" or "somatic" element, finally, is manifested in Islam in the form of an opaque and flat obedientialism, which incidentally — since it exists — penetrates even into, theology,[5] for example when we are assured that good is

---

4. In the case of Christians, the *kshatriya* element dominates in theology, whereas that of the *vaishya* can be felt in the sector of lay morality, which is condemned in advance to a certain mediocrity. The *kshatriya* mentality moreover had its share in provoking, within Christianity, two divergent explosions, the Renaissance and the Reformation; it was a factor both of idealism and unrealism, of impulse and of instability. The Islamic *upāya* sought to avoid this pitfall, which it could do only at the price of new risks.

5. In Christianity, the equivalent of this *shūdra* piety is blind, irrational and absurd humilitarism, but obviously ennobled by its intention. The point here is not to condemn, but to state and to define; if the *shūdra* mentality has a role to play in religion, it is because the very ideas of "servitude" (Islam) and of "sin" (Christianity) paradoxically give it a completely natural right to be present, especially since every man carries within himself all potentialities; it is the levelling and pessimistic moralisms that insist upon it, precisely.

good and evil and evil, because God so decided and for no other reason; or that God rewards the good and punishes the bad without our being able to know why, for He would be "free" to do the opposite; and that we must believe obvious things, not because our mind finds them obvious — for obviousness would limit the "freedom" and the "sovereignty" of God — but for the sole reason that God has thus informed us without our having the right to the least need for causality; in short, when everything is made to depend upon a divine arbitrariness which is unintelligible by definition and to which our will, and even our intelligence, have merely to yield, as if in such conditions it were still worthwhile being man.

The accent that Islam puts on the horizontal mentality — the prudent and realistic mentality of businessmen and caravaneers, if one will, accompanied of course by warrior qualities — is explained by the concern to speak to the average man and to save the largest number possible; in the last analysis, consequently, it is a manifestation of Mercy. Through the average man, necessarily "horizontal" in certain respects, the Islamic *upāya* seeks to reach every man as such.

For this is inescapable: the masses, to capture whom is the mission of religion, seek to recognize themselves in it, which forces religion to prefigure them in a certain way, on pain of being unfaithful to its mandate. God Himself in His Mercy condescends to assume some aspects of those He would save, so that they may recognize themselves in Him, otherwise no dialogue would be possible.

*

* *

It will perhaps be worthwhile to further describe the characteristics of the *vaishya*,[6] since these characteristics

6. In the European *vaishya*, the elements "peasant" and "craftsman" predominate over the element "merchant," whereas in the Near-Easterner the relationship is inverse. Let us add that in the case of the

insinuate themselves into the moralistic and sentimental *karma-mārga* of the Semitic religions and consequently are found abusively amalgamated with the esoterism of the Sufis; unless one gives up trying to define Sufism as a whole as an esoterism and situates the latter in a very inward and very implicit sector. Thus, the characteristics of the *vaishya* are *grosso modo* the following: love of work well done — as regards both the result and the performance — and of wages honestly earned; an emotional accent placed on the fear of God and on meritorious works, conscientiously and piously accomplished; whence also, in matters of piety, a "top of the class" zeal coupled with an occasional tendency to platitude and pedantry; an intelligence solid enough in its own way, but above all modest, practical and circumspect.[7] On the speculative plane, which is scarcely his, the *vaishya* lacks realism, as if he wished to compensate for his horizontality by an escape into the clouds; thus he readily puts the sublime in the place of the true or the real, if indeed he ventures into the world of religious speculation, which no one can prevent him from doing.[8]

It is in the logic of things that a religion or a spiritual .

great artist — unless he be "noble" or "priest" by heredity — his quality as craftsman is no longer a merely outward one, and it rejoins by its inward quality the chivalrous and sacerdotal mentalities; this brings us to the obvious point that a member of a lower collectivity can belong individually to a higher collectivity, and vice versa, whatever be the outward function of the individual.

7. *Quidquid agis, prudenter agas, et respice finem*: "Whatever thou doest, do it prudently, and think of the end." This medieval saying, no doubt inspired by Ecclesiastes, reflects well the "horizontal," precautionary and perfectionistic mentality in question.

8. A factor that attenuates and may even abolish these generalizations is the fact that each of the castes contains the others in an appropriate manner. Let us also note that each caste — each qualitative type — contains the four temperaments, the order of the castes being vertical, and that of the temperaments, horizontal; this implies that each mental level comprises features that are both characteristic and divergent.

101

method, to the extent that it stresses the importance of outward observances,[9] assumes in its human substance a psychology in conformity with the one we have just described; for if the *vaishya* tends to be narrowly moralistic through lack of a sense of proportions, every pedantic moralist is *ipso facto* situated at the same level, whatever be his latent possibilities.

As a complement to pious agitation, there is pious contraction, the gaze timorously and chastely cast to the ground; notwithstanding the acceptance — in another dimension — of "legal"[10] enjoyments. We would not contest the possible value of such attitudes, for differing mental-

9. We must be clear about the meaning of the term "outward observances." When one follows the Sunna for the most contingent actions of daily life or when one recites the formulas appropriate to the most trivial situations, one practices "outward" or "secondary" observances; but when one performs a rite whose content is essential, this rite is not "outward" simply because it is performed physically. We have read somewhere in the writings of Omar Suhrawardī the story of a Sufi who, sensing that he was dying, wished for one last time to perform the ritual ablution so as to appear before God in a state of "legal purity"; not having the strength to carry out this final act, he took the hand of one of those present to perform with it the missing act. We do not say that he was wrong from his point of view; but we say that this point of view is not everything; and we would say — no doubt a little schematically — that a Hindu in his situation would have pronounced a *mantra* or a *nāma*, which purifies from all defilement and constitutes a central sacrament, and is thus a qualitatively "inward" practice. Ramakrishna tells the story of a holy *brāhmana* who asked a *shūdra* near a well to draw some water for him; the man did not dare to do so because of his impurity of caste. "Say *Shiva*," replied the *brāhmana*, "and you will be pure." And let us recall that the *Bhagavadgītā* specifies that "there is no lustral water like unto Knowledge."

10. Without forgetting more subtle cases and without seeking to be displeasingly schematic, the following remarks are called for: it is logical that man should be chastely apprehensive to the extent that his sense of pleasure is opaque and quantitative; certain *ahādīth* on Paradise, along with the accompanying speculations, collide with this opaqueness. This perhaps constitutes an attenuating circumstance for the Sufis who will not hear tell of the "Garden" and what it contains, in spite of all that is hasty and ill-sounding in their point of view.

102

ities have their requirements as they have their limits, but we are compelled to criticize them when they become excessive or when they are presented as the only possible perfections, or as perfection in itself. Let all this be said without forgetting that every man carries within himself possibilities inferior to his overall possibility, and that there can always be circumstances in which he must take account of these in a concrete fashion; no man can conduct himself carelessly like a god.

A striking aspect of the "horizontality" of the *vaishya* is his conventionalism, which may take the place of a more or less direct vision of things. Conventionalism is a safeguard against the lack of a sense of proportions for those who are not sufficiently endowed with discernment; whence the advantages of even a blind practice of the integral Sunna. The weight of "conventions" is useful, when required, in men of high caste who, although contemplatives, may lack discrimination:[11] convention provides a sure framework for their mystical impulses which may be too colored by individualism, thus preventing extravagant consequences on the social level; it then serves as an anchor, and as a normative criterion, in the coming-and-going of inspirations that are difficult to verify.

*

*　*

No doubt it is not only the inward that counts, there is also the outward; there are not merely great things, there are also small things; Moslems insist on this, and rightly so as long as they do not dramatize in favor of a disproportionate and invasive *karma-mārga*.[12] Rightly so, we say, but let no one tell us that the quantity and affective in-

---

11. Throughout we are speaking of personal caste, and not necessarily of social caste.

12. We use the term *karma-mārga* in a special and restricted sense for in Hinduism the "way of works" can be much more than that; it is even above all — at the level of the *kshatriyas* — the accomplishment of

tensity of observances practically constitute esoterism or lead to Supreme Knowledge; or that bigoted agitation is an integral part of the sapiential way or even practically constitutes gnosis.

Leaving aside its escesses, exteriorizing moralism is no doubt founded on the idea that since the loss of Paradise everyone carries within himself inferior elements; in fact, all believers participate in the same observances — although assuredly they comprise certain margins — but this does not mean that because of this loss everyone is a *vaishya* or *shūdra*; it is incumbent upon traditional wisdom, be it exoteric or esoteric, not to overlook just lines of demarcation. The enigma of the Arabo-Moslem soul being a certain mixture, as well as a certain conflict, between the mentality of the "knight" and that of the "merchant" — the heroism which charges and if need be simplifies, and the prudence which evalutes and readily overemphasizes details — it is not surprising that certain lines of demarcation be particularly shifting, and that the esoteric domain be affected thereby.

A possible objection is the following: the esoteric perspectives of love and knowledge must be protected against any usurpation of their privileges of inwardness and essentiality; consequently, esoterism itself is obliged to set up a barrier composed of pious outwardness, and thus exclude any temptation towards ambition and hypocrisy. All very well; but the whole question is to know where one wishes to situate the boundary between this concern for integrity and the adulteration of esoterism. The man who

---

the duty pertaining to one's function, without attachment to the fruit of the works *(nishkāma-karma)*, which proves moreover that the simple fact of practicing multiple outward observances does not constitute in itself a phenomenon of outwardness or of a horizontal mentality. — As for the cult of small outward observances, it is certainly also pronounced in Judaism, but here it takes on a less personalistic and less sentimental character than in Islam. No Jew would ask himself how Moses sat down in order to eat grapes.

is qualified, it will be said, will find his way; "God knows his own." And let us hope that this is sufficient consolation in the face of so much ambiguity!

Another objection might be based on the psychological influence of the *ahādīth*, and thus of the Sunna; for it is from them that is derived the meticulous and fussy *karma-yoga* that so often veils, sometimes in such an impenetrable way, esoterism properly so-called. It is readily forgotten that, in providing rules for living and in doing so in detail, the Prophet did not say that this was supreme wisdom; moreover, the responsibility for these compilations does not fall upon the Prophet himself—who in many cases merely acted in his own manner—but on his Companions, who sought to conserve the least gesture and the least remark of the Prophet and who did so with all the dryness and all the meticulousness of which the Arabs are capable, to the point of not always being able to avoid a certain "pettiness," if this word be permitted in a matter of this kind. The Koran says that in order to be loved by God, we must follow the Prophet; the Companions deduced from this that the integral example of the Prophet is a sort of sacrament, a sort of sanctifying and saving mold into which one must flow without concerning oneself with the why of things.[13] If, on the one hand, the *ahādīth* and the accounts connected with them often give the impression of pettiness because of their content, either because too modest or too human—we have in mind for example some of the stories regarding the Prophet's wives —nevertheless on the other hand the very existence of the *adādīth* bears witness to an extraordinary cause; for the fact that one has taken the trouble religiously to collect the

---

13. Completely different is the Christian point of view; St. John, indeed far from compiling "information" *(hadīth, ahādīth)*, limits himself to the essential: "There are also many other things which Jesus did, the which, if they should be written every one, I suppose that even the world itself could not contain the books that should be written."

105

least gestures of a man proves the immensity of his prestige and the greatness of his nature. The argument that the way of multiple observances and of their mystical accentuation is the exclusive way of the Prophet, is perfectly abusive, for every founder of a religion inevitably provides an example of all kinds of attitudes and ways of acting, without this constituting his message properly socalled; and the fact that these manifestations can contradict one another proves precisely that they constitute a choice and that no single one of them totally or exclusively involves the authority of the Messenger.

It is true that the meticulous imitation of the slightest deeds and gestures of the Prophet, the scrupulous and extinctive entering into the mold of his person, is a sort of eucharistic participation in the man-Logos; nevertheless this participation is limited to the plane of the individuality and assumes importance to the extent that the way is that of the individual, something that has no direct connection with metaphysical realization. The latter, certainly, does not exclude this imitation, to be sure, but on the one hand simplifies it and on the other interiorizes it; the spiritual accentuation in this case being beyond the human realm.

In any case, if an outward activity, however multiple, is in itself reconcilable with a methodic contemplation of the Essence—of the "Kingdom of God which is within you"—the same is not true of an individualistic and exteriorizing accentuation of numerous observances, for this is a quantitative search for personal merits; the accentuation of the individual and the outward necessarily excludes that of the universal and the inward.[14] What is blameworthy is not pious pettiness and its fragmentariness, but its claim—when present—to totality and greatness.

But let us return to a more general consideration. The

14. Clearly, the anecdotes pertaining to this *distinguo* are not lacking in Sufism.

Sunna seeks to keep in mind the security, equilibrium and sincerity of the man who knows he is little, whereas the Christian perspective has in view first and foremost inward values, as well as the risks of the ideal and of heroism. It goes without saying that each of the two ways of seeing includes *a posteriori* and to a certain degree the perspective of the other; Christians have their monastic rules and their courtesy, just as Moslems for their part have their anti-social and, when necessary, anti-ritualistic idealism; this second epithet concerning at least supererogatory practices. "And the remembrance of God is greater," says the Koran; greater than the canonical prayer, and consequently, in principle, greater than all observances.[15]

*
* *

We should like to provide a few supplementary details regarding the hierarchy of the fundamental human mentalities, always employing — because it is more convenient — Hindu terminology despite the Islamic context; and we do so without scruple, since the nature of things has no denominational coloring.

What the two higher castes have in common — we are speaking of typological castes, not of social castes, still less of classes — is acuity of intelligence, the capacity spontaneously to place oneself above oneself; hence the predominance of the qualitative over the quantitative and, in spirituality, the accentuation of inwardness and verticality, whether it be a question of wisdom or of heroism. On the contrary, what unfavorably characterizes the third caste — leaving aside, that is, its qualities — is a mentality that is more or less mercantile, or let us say a certain intellectual and moral pettiness due to outwardness and hori-

15. Likewise the remembrance of God is the reason for the existence of every rite and every practice, as the Shaykh Al-'Alawī remarked in one of his treatises.

zontality;[16] but as regards the fourth caste, the third has in common with the first two an inward incentive towards the good, whereas the fourth cannot maintain itself in the good except under a pressure that comes from outside and above, for this human type is not dominated by itself and does not like to dominate itself. Finally, what the second and the third castes—and still more so the fourth—have in common, is a certain "worldliness," but in extremely different respects.

Compared with the outcastes, who because of their heterogeneous psychic make-up and their lack of a center are "out of balance," the four normal and normative types are "well-balanced": amongst the four castes, the first three types can be said to be "disciplined," and amongst these three the first two types can be said to be "noble." We do not mean "nobility" in the sociological sense of the term, but in the sense that the spirit is "free," and thus "sovereign," because naturally in conformity with the Universal Law, whether this conformity be in "heroic" or in "sacral" mode; man is noble to the extent that he carries the Law within himself; in other cases, he is ennobled to the extent that his obedience is perfect, and to the extent that, having been quantitative, it becomes qualitative.

If on the one hand the *brāhmana* and the *kshatriya* are close to one another by their superior intelligence and by the authority that springs from it, on the other hand there is a meeting point between the *brāhmana* and the *vaishya* from the fact that both are pacific, and from the fact that the second possesses a certain contemplativity which also relates him to the first. It is easy to see the pacific character of the peasant, the craftsman, the merchant; none of them has any interest in coming to blows and each of the

16. It could also be said that this mentality looks upon the whole from the starting point of the details—whence its specific moralism— whereas the higher mentality looks upon the details from the starting point of the whole. In the first case, analysis takes precedence over synthesis; in the second, synthesis takes precedence over analysis.

three functions possesses an aspect that binds or unites human groups rather than opposes them; as for contemplativity it results, in the case of the peasant, from his life in nature, in the case of the craftsman, from his preoccupation with symbolism and the sacred; in the case of the merchant, from his constant contact with useful and beautiful objects whose worth he knows, and in this respect he is disinterested, which he shows by his perspicacity and his honesty.[17] All in all, the pacific and contemplative *vaishya* is morally and spiritually superior to a *kshatriya* who is merely ambitious and quarrelsome;[18] although the *kshatriya* is in himself superior by his liveliness of intelligence, strength of decision, and heroic vocation. The pitfall of the *kshatriya* spirit is an intelligence with too little contemplativeness; that of the *vaishya* a contemplativity with too little intelligence; but it is the objective content that counts, not the subjective appearance.

In the same line of compensatory phenomena, we must call attention to a possible superiority of the *kshatriya*, not over the *brāhmana* in himself and as sage, of course, but over the professional priest who has become narrow and pedantic, even pharisaic, through "specialization."[19] On the other hand, the *brāhmana* in the absolute sense eminently possesses all the capacities of the *kshatriya*,[20] which is not true of the functional and social *brāh-*

17. The important role of the *vaishya* spirit in Islam — and let us not forget that Islam is a world religion and not a brotherhood of gnostics — is prefigured in the fact that the Prophet married a rich business-woman, and was himself employed in business before his prophetic career.

18. "Blessed are the peacemakers, for they shall be called the children of God": these words of Jesus, apart from their general meaning, apply both to the *brāhmana* and to the *vaishya*, in respect of their affinity.

19. In the West, the emperor, and with him the other princes, were often more realistic than the clergy, including the pope; as Danta well knew.

20. Pharaoh in Egypt, as well as the emperors of China and

mana; in other words the intrinsic *brāhmana* is *ativarna*, "without color" (of caste), and he is thus identifiable with the *hamsa*, the primordial man.[21]

We spoke above of the pacific nature that is common to the first and third castes, and we should like to add the following: if Islam is a doctrine of the *brāhmana* vehicled by a piety of the *vaishya*—the *kshatriya* element not being predominant overall—it is precisely by reason of its being rooted in the mystery of Peace *(Salām)*, which includes *a priori* the sage, but paradoxically also the small and the weak. Islam is itself an invitation to "appeasement," in the sense that the root of the word *islām* is the same as that of the word *salām*: "to resign oneself" or "to surrender" *(as-lama)*, is to be reintegrated into "Peace," which is an aspect of God. *As-Salām* is one of the ninety-nine Divine Names.[22] "And God calleth to the abode of Peace *(dar as-Salām)* and guideth whom He will on the straight path."[23]

*

*   *

According to the Koran, man is essentially two things: "servant" *('abd)* and "vicar" *(khalīfah)*: and not "servant" exclusively as a "quantitative" and ill-inspired piety would have it. The Prophet is both "servant" and "messenger"

Japan, sought to realize this primordial synthesis; but a little belatedly.

21. The saint withdrawn from the world, the *sannyāssī*, is said to be "beyond-caste," *ativarna*: this characteristic amounts to primordial wisdom, *sophia perennis*, and thus to esoterism. If every saint is personally a *brāhmana* from the simple fact of his sanctity, even though socially he be a pariah like Tiruvalluvar, every sage sharing in the *sophia perennis* is *ativarna*, beyond caste. We would add that the *brāhmana*-priest may be bound by his form and his function, whereas the *ativarnāshrāmī*, as such and in principle, is neither limited nor bound by anything exterior to him.

22. Likewise the blessed in Paradise utter no "vain or harmful" word, but only the words: *Salāman Salāmā (Sura of the Inevitable Event, 25-26)*.

23. *Sura Yūnus, 25.*

(*rasūl*), not one without the other, which ought to be enough to let us recognize in the man who believes, the dignity which he possesses by definition, and which results from his deiformity: we say "in the man who believes," for the dignity of "vicar" is dependent upon the consent of the individual to the specific vocation of man.

We referred above to the leveling that is comprised in exoterism. Exoterist "reasoning" is on the whole as follows: it is necessary to be able to save all men, including the most earthbound, and since these are the most difficult to save, it is necessary to adapt to their needs more than to those of others; and consequently, all men must to some extent be *shūdras*. From this arises all too often the paradox of a spirituality that applies to all a psychology — and imposes on all a morality — of *vaishyas* and *shūdras*, whereas it is precisely in this domain that the distinction of the human levels is most necessary; let us recall in this connection the gnostic distinction between the *pneumatikos*, the *psychikos* and the *hylikos*.[24]

In respect of their status as responsible, free and weak individuals, men are equal before the saving Law; in respect of their supra-individual participation in the immanent Intellect, which is also saving, they are unequal. The first respect concerns exoterism, and the second esoterism: the latter fully accepts, and even requires, the submission of the individual to the Law; of the individual,

---

24. To this it might be objected that before God every man is a *shūdra*, which is both true and false; it is true in a transposed sense which removes from the word its psychological implication, and it is false because of this very reservation. Referring to a *hadīth* that condemns all rich men to hell, Ibn 'Arabī declares that this remark applies only to crude people who are attached to their riches, and not to sages who know for themselves that it is not to be taken literally. This opinion shows that there are sayings that concern only a given moral or intellectual level, and that there is no question, especially from the Sufi point of view, of reducing all men to a single rudimentary type; nevertheless this error is frequently committed, and precisely on the basis of canonical formulations.

but not of that within him which pertains to the Intellect.
The Intellect is the Law of the microcosm, just as the Law
is the Intellect of the macrocosm; there is parallelism, in
keeping with what is required by the nature of things, but
not confusion.[25]

In fact, the term "Sufism" includes the most shallow
fanaticism as well as the most profound speculation; now
neither one nor the other constitutes total *Tasawwuf,*
which goes without saying in the case of the first attitude,
whereas the second is integral esoterism only on condition
that it be accompanied by an appropriate method and not
merely by pious observances, whose emotional accentuation moreover is scarcely compatible with the perspective
of gnosis. Authentic esoterism—let us say it again—is the
way which is founded on total or essential truth, and not
merely on partial or formal truth, and which makes an
operative use of the intelligence, and not only of the will
and the feelings. The totality of truth demands the totality
of man.

25. According to the *Brahma Sūtras* (III, 4: 36-38), "man can ac-
quire Knowledge even without observing the prescribed rites: and in
fact one finds in the *Vēda* many examples of people who failed to ac-
complish particular rites, or who were prevented from so doing, and
who, nevertheless, because their attention was perpetually fixed on
the Supreme *Brahma,* acquired the true Knowledge that concerns It."
Likewise, Shankara in his *Atmā-Bodha:* "There is no other means of
obtaining complete and final Deliverance than by Knowledge, this
alone removes the bonds of the passions . . . Action *(karma),* not being opposed to ignorance *(avidyā),* cannot remove it; but Knowledge
dissipates ignorance, just as light dissipates darkness."—Such remarks concern only "pneumatics"; now the fact that the majority of
pneumatics practiced certain actions—ritual, moral or other—does
not mean that they were ignorant of the relative character of action,
nor still more so that they attained Knowledge by means of action;
and if a given *hadīth* appears to make mystical Union dependent on
supererogatory acts, this is solely because it takes as its starting-point
the tendencies of exteriorized man, not to mention the fact that certain rites can be supports for cognitive actualization. Action collaborates with intellection and contemplation, but does not replace them,
nor is it a *conditio sine qua non.*

Human Premises of a Religious Dilemma

We have seen that the ransom of the providential levelling realized by Islam is a certain predominance of the
vaishya spirit,[26] a spirit which is so paradoxical in a Sufic
climate, but which has contributed to sparing Islam a
luciferian experience analogous to the Renaissance; nevertheless this unquestionably simplistic mentality tends to
produce in Moslems, on contact with the modern world,
an aberrant intellectualistic reaction and finally apostasy.
This for us is one more reason for describing without
euphemism the disadvantages of the levelling in question,
so as to be able to point out its occasionally attenuating or
compensatory causes, and above all so as to be able to
demonstrate its relativity in the face of the essential and
decisive values of Tradition.

26. "A fusion of the elect and the general, the Islamic aristo-de-
mocracy can be effected without violence or promiscuity thanks to the
peculiarly Islamic institution of a conventional type of humanity,
which, for want of a better term, I shall call, average man or human
normality . . . It is precisely the 'average man' who is the object of the
Shari'ah or the sacred Law of Islam . . . Certain Sharaite prescriptions
may seem absurd in the eyes of Europeans. They nevertheless have
their reason for existence. A universal religion must reckon with
every intellectual and moral degree. The simplicity, weaknesses, and
peculiarities of other people have, to a certain extent, a right to consideration. But intellectual culture also has its rights and its requirements. The average man sets up around each person a sort of neutral-
ity which guarantees all individualities, while obliging them to work
for the whole of (Moslem) humanity." (Abdul-Hādī, "L'universalité
en l'Islam," in *Le Voile d'Isis*, January 1934.).

CHAPTER 5

Tracing the Notion of Philosophy

Were Ibn 'Arabī, Jīlī and other theoreticians of Sufism philosophers? Yes and no, depending on the meaning given to this word.

According to Pythagoras, wisdom is *a priori* the knowledge of the stellar world and of all that is situated above us; *sophia* being the wisdom of the gods, and *philosophia* that of men. For Heraclitus, the philosopher is one who applies himself to the knowledge of the profound nature of things; whereas for Plato, philosophy is the knowledge of the Immutable and of the Ideas; and for Aristotle, it is the knowledge of first causes and principles, together with the sciences that are derived from them. In addition, philosophy implies for all of the Ancients moral conformity to wisdom: only he is wise, *sophos*, who lives wisely. In this particular and precise sense, the wisdom of Solomon is philosophy; it is to live according to the nature of things, on the basis of piety — of the "fear of God" — with a view to that which is essential and liberating.

All this shows that, to say the least, the word "philosopher" in itself has nothing restrictive about it, and that one cannot legitimately impute to this word any of the vexing associations of ideas that it may elicit; usage applies this word to all thinkers, including eminent metaphysicians — some Sufis consider Plato and other Greeks to be prophets — so that one would like to reserve it for sages and simply use the term "rationalists" for profane thinkers. It is nevertheless legitimate to take account of a misuse of language that has become conventional, for unquestionably the terms "philosophy" and "philosopher" have been seriously compromised by ancient and modern reasoners; in fact, the serious inconvenience of these terms is that they conventionally imply that the norm for the mind is reasoning pure and simple,[1] in the absence, not only of intellection, but also of indispensable objective data. Admittedly one is neither ignorant nor rationalistic just because one is a logician, but one is both if one is a logician and nothing more.[2]

In the opinion of all profane thinkers, philosophy means to think "freely," as far as possible without presuppositions, which precisely is impossible; on the other hand, gnosis, or philosophy in the proper and primitive sense of the word, is to think in accordance with the immanent Intellect and not by means of reason alone. What favors confusion is the fact that in both cases the intelligence operates independently of outward prescriptions, although for diametrically opposed reasons: that the rationalist if need be draws his inspiration from a pre-existing system does not prevent him from thinking in a way that he deems to be "free"—falsely, since true freedom coincides with truth—likewise, *mutatis mutandis*: that the gnostic—in the orthodox sense of the term—bases himself

1. Naturally the most "advanced" of the modernists seek to demolish the very principles of reasoning, but this is simply fantasy *pro domo*, for man is condemned to reason as soon as he uses language, unless he wishes to demonstrate nothing at all. In any case, one cannot demonstrate the impossibility of demonstrating anything, if words are still to have any meaning.

2. A German author (H. Türck) has proposed the term "misosopher"—"enemy of wisdom"—for those thinkers who undermine the very foundations of truth and intelligence. We will add that misosophy—without mentioning some ancient precedents—begins *grosso modo* with "criticism" and ends with subjectivisms, relativisms, existentialisms, dynamisms, psychologisms and biologisms of every kind. As for the ancient expression "misology," it designates above all the hatred of the fideist for the use of reason.

extrinsically on a given sacred Scripture or on some other gnostic cannot prevent him from thinking in an intrinsically free manner by virtue of the freedom proper to the immanent Truth, or proper to the Essence which by definition escapes formal constraints. Or again: whether the gnostic "thinks" what he has "seen" with the "eye of the heart," or whether on the contrary he obtains his "vision" thanks to the intervention—preliminary and provisional and in no wise efficient—of a thought which then takes on the role of occasional cause, is a matter of indifference with regard to the truth, or with regard to its almost supernatural springing forth in the spirit.

*

* *

The reduction of the notion of intellectuality to that of simple rationality often has its cause in the prejudice of a school: St. Thomas is a sensationalist—that is to say he reduces the cause of all non-theological knowledge to sensible perceptions—in order to be able to underestimate the human mind to the advantage of Scripture; in other words, because this allows him to attribute to Revelation alone the glory of "supernatural" knowledge. And Ghazālī inveighs against the "philosophers" because he wishes to reserve for the Sufis the monopoly of spiritual knowledge, as if faith and piety, combined with intellectual gifts and grace—all the Arab philosophers were believers—did not provide a sufficient basis for pure intellection.

According to Ibn 'Arabī, the "philosopher"—which for him practically means the skeptic—is incapable of knowing universal causality except by observing causations in the outward world and by drawing from his observations the conclusions that impose themselves on his sense of logic. According to another Sufi, Ibn al-'Arīf, intellectual knowledge is only an "indication" pointing to God: the philosopher only knows God by way of a "conclusion," his knowledge only has a content "with a view to God," and

117

not "by God" as does that of the mystic. But this *distinguo* is only valid, as we have said, if we assimilate all philosophy to unmitigated rationalism and forget in addition that in the doctrinaire mystics there is an obvious element of rationality. In short, the term "philosopher" in current speech signifies nothing other than the fact of expounding a doctrine while respecting the laws of logic, which are those of language and those of common sense, without which we would not be human; to practice philosophy is first and foremost to think, whatever may be the reasons which rightly or wrongly incite us to do so. But it is also, more especially and according to the best of the Greeks, to express by means of the reason certainties "seen" or "lived" by the immanent Intellect, as we have remarked above; now the explanation necessarily takes on the character imposed on it by the laws of thought and language.

Some will object that the simple believer who understands nothing of philosophy can derive much more from scriptural symbols than does the philosopher with his definitions, abstractions, classifications and categories; an unjust reproach, for theorizing thought firstly does not exclude supra-rational intuition — which is completely obvious — and secondly does not pretend to provide by itself anything that it cannot offer by virtue of its nature. This something may be of immense value, otherwise it would be necessary to suppress all doctrines; platonic *anamnesis* can have as occasional cause doctrinal concepts as well as symbols provided by art or virgin nature. If in intellectual speculation there is a human danger of rationalism, and thus — at least in principle — of skepticism and materialism, mystical speculation for its part comprises, with the same reservation, a danger of excesses, or even of rambling and incoherence, whatever may be said by the esoterizing zealots who take pleasure in question-begging and sublimizing euphemisms.

*

* *

118

We have to say a few words here in defense of the Arab philosophers who have been accused, amongst other things, of confusing Plato, Aristotle and Plotinus. We consider that, on the contrary, they had the merit of integrating these great Greeks in one and the same synthesis, for what interested them was not systems, but truth in itself. We shall no doubt run counter to certain esoterist prejudices if we say that metaphysically orthodox philosophy — that of the Middle Ages as well as of antiquity — pertains to sapiential esoterism, either intrinsically by its truth, or extrinsically with regard to the simplifications of theology; it is "thinking," if one will, but not ratiocination in the void. If it be objected that the errors that one may find in some philosophers who overall are orthodox prove the non-esoteric and consequently profane nature of all philosophy, this argument can be turned against theology and the mystical or gnostic doctrines, for in these sectors erroneous speculations can also be found on the margin of real inspirations.

To give a concrete example, we shall mention the following case, which in any event is interesting in itself and apart from any question of terminology: the Arab philosophers rightly accept the eternity of the world for, as they say, God cannot create at a given moment without putting Himself in contradiction with his very nature, and thus without absurdity;[3] most ingeniously Ghazālī replies — and others have repeated the same argument — that there is no "before" with regard to creation, that time "was" created with, for and in the world. Now this argument is invalid since it is unilateral: for if it safeguards the transcendence, the absolute freedom and the timelessness of the Creator with regard to creation, it does not explain the temporality of the latter; which is to say that it does

3. Indeed the unicity of God excludes that of the world, in succession as well as in extent; the infinity of God demands the repetition of the world, in both respects: creation cannot be a unique event, anymore than it can be reduced to the human world alone.

119

not take account of the temporal limitation of a unique world projected into the void of non-time, a limitation which engages God since He is its cause and since it exists in relation to His eternity;[4] the very nature of duration demands a beginning. The solution of the problem is that the co-eternity of the world is not that of our "actual" world — which of necessity had an origin and will have an end — but that this co-eternity consists in the necessity of successive worlds: God being what He is — with His absolute Necessity and His absolute Freedom — He cannot not create necessarily, but He is free in the modes of creation, which never repeat themselves since God is infinite. The whole difficulty comes from the fact that the Semites envisage only one world, namely ours, whereas the non-Semiticized Aryans either accept an indefinite series of creations — this is the Hindu doctrine of cosmic cycles — or else envisage the world as the necessary manifestation of the Divine Nature and not as a contingent and particular phenomenon. In this confrontation between two theses, the theological and the philosophical, it is the philosophers and not the theologians — even it they were Sufis like Ghazālī — who are right; and if doctrinal esoterism is the explanation of problems posed but not clarified by faith, we do not see why those philosophers who provide

---

4. All the same, there is in favor of this argument — which moreover is repeated by Ibn 'Arabī — the attenuating circumstance that it is the only way of reconciling the emanationist truth with the creationist dogma without giving the latter an interpretation too far removed from the "letter"; we say "emanationist truth" in order to emphasize that it is a question of the authentic metaphysical idea and not of some pantheistic or deistic emanationism. Be that as it may, Ibn 'Arabī, when speaking of creation — at the beginning of his *Fusūs al-Hikam* — cannot help expressing himself in temporal mode: "When the Divine Real willed to see . . . its Essence" (*lammā shā'a'l-Haqqu subhānahu an yarā . . . 'aynahu . . .*); it is true that in Arabic the past tense has in principle the sense of the eternal present when it is a question of God, but this applies above all to the verb "to be" (*kāna*) and does not prevent creation from being envisaged as an "act" and not as a "quality."

this explanation thanks to intellection—for reasoning pure and simple would not succeed in doing so, and it is moreover metaphysical truth that proves the worth of the intuition corresponding to it—do not have the same merit as the recognized esoterists, especially since, to paraphrase St. Paul, one cannot testify to great truths except by the Holy Spirit.

For the theologians, to say that the world is "without beginning" amounts to saying that it is eternal *a se*—this is why they reject the idea—whereas for the philosophers it means that it is eternal *ab alio,* for it is God who lends it eternity. Now an eternity that is lent is a completely different thing from eternity in itself, and it is precisely for this reason that the world is both eternal and temporal: eternal as a series of creations or a creative rhythm, and temporal by the fact that each link in this flux has a beginning and an end. It is Universal Manifestation in itself that is co-eternal with God because it is a necessary expression of His eternal Nature—the sun being unable to abstain from shining—but eternity cannot be reduced to a given contingent phase of this divine Manifestation. Manifestation is "co-eternal," that is: not eternal, as only the Essence is; and this is why it is periodically interrupted and totally re-absorbed into the Principle, so much so that it is both existent and inexistent, and does not enjoy a plenary and so to speak "continuous" reality like the Eternal itself. To say that the world is "co-eternal" nevertheless means that it is necessary as an aspect of the Principle, that it is therefore "something of God," which is already indicated by the term "Manifestation"; and it is precisely this truth that the theologians refuse to accept; for obvious reasons since in their eyes it abolishes the difference between creature and Creator.[5]

5. The total Universe can be compared either to a circle or to a cross, the center in both cases representing the Principle; but whereas in the first image the relationship between the periphery and the center is discontinuous, this being the dogmatist perspective of theology,

The "co-eternity" of the world with God evokes the universal *Materia* of Empedocles and Ibn Masarrah, which is none other than the Logos as Substance (*amā* = "cloud" or *habā* = "dust"):[6] it is not creation as such that is co-eternal with the Creator, it is the creative virtuality, which comprises — according to these doctrines — four fundamental formative principles. These are, symbolically speaking, "Fire," "Air," "Water," "Earth,"[7] which recall the three principial determinations *(gunas)* included in *Prakriti*: *Sattva, Rajas, Tamas*; the difference in number indicating a secondary difference in perspective.[8]

*

*　*

As regards the confrontation between Sufis and philosophers, the following remark must be made: if Ghazālī had limited himself to asserting that there is no possible esoteric realization without an initiation and a corresponding method, and that the philosophers in general

---

analogically speaking, in the second image the same relationship is continuous, this being the perspective of gnosis. The first perspective is valid when phenomena as such are envisaged — something that gnosis would not contest — whereas the second perspective adequately takes account of the essential reality of things and of the Universe.

6. This idea, like the terms used to express it, belongs to Islam, apart from the Greek analogies noted later; there is nothing surprising in this, since truth is one.

7. This Empedoclean quaternity is found in another form in the cosmology of the Indians of North American, and perhaps also of Mexico and other more southern regions: here it is Space that symbolizes Substance, the universal "Ether," while the cardinal points represent the four principial and existentiating determinations.

8. *Sattva* — analogically speaking — is the "Fire" which rises and illumines; *Tamas* is then the "Earth" which is heavy and obscure. *Rajas* — by reason of its intermediary position — comprises an aspect of lightness and another of heaviness, namely "Air" and "Water," but both envisaged in violent mode: on the one hand it is the unleashing of the winds and on the other that of the waves.

demand neither the one nor the other,[9] we would have no reason to reproach him; but his criticism is levelled at philosophy as such, that is to say, it is situated above all on the doctrinal and epistemological plane. In fact, the Hellenizing philosophy that is in question here is neutral from the initiatic point of view, given that its intention is to provide an exposition of the truth, and nothing else; particular opinions — such as rationalism properly so-called — do not enter into the definition of philosophy.[10] Be that as it may, Ghazālī's ostracism makes us think of those ancient theologians who sought to oppose the "vain wisdom of the world" with the "tears of repentance," but who finally did not refrain from constructing systems of their own, and in doing so could not do without the help of the Greeks, to whom nevertheless they denied the assistance of the "Holy Spirit" and therefore any supernatural quality.

The Sufis do not wish to be philosophers, that is understood; and they are right if they mean by this that their starting point is not doubt and that their certainties are not rational conclusions. But we absolutely do not see why, when they reason wrongly they would do so in a manner different from the philosophers; nor why a philosopher, when he conceives a truth whose transcendent and

9. This possible silence proves nothing in any case against the rightness of a given philosophy; Plato said moreover in one of his letters that his writings did not include all of his teachings. It may be noted that according to Synesius the goal of monks and philosophers is the same, namely the contemplation of God.

10. In our first book, *The Transcendent Unity of Religions*, we adopted the point of view of Ghazālī regarding "philosophy": that is to say, bearing in mind the great impoverishment of modern philosophies, we simplified the problem, as others have done before us, by making "philosophy" synonymous with "rationalism." According to Ghazālī, to practice philosophy is to operate by syllogisms — but he cannot do without them himself — and thus to use logic; the question remains whether one does so *a priori* or *a posteriori*.

axiomatic nature he recognizes, would do so in a manner different from the Sufis.

It was not as a gnostic but as a "thinker" that Ibn 'Arabī treated the question of evil, explaining it by subjectivity and relativity, with an entirely Pyrrhonic logic. What is serious is that in practically abolishing evil — since it is reduced to a subjective point of view — one abolishes with the same stroke good, whether this was the intention or not; and in particular one abolishes beauty by depriving love of its content, whereas it is precisely on their reality and their necessary connection that Ibn 'Arabī's doctrine insists. It is beauty that determines love, not inversely: the beautiful is not what we love and because we love it, but that which by its objective value obliges us to love it; we love the beautiful because it is beautiful, even if in fact it may happen that we lack judgement, which does not invalidate the principle of the normal relationship between object and subject. Likewise, the fact that one may love because of an inward beauty and in spite of an outward ugliness, or that love may be mixed with compassion or other indirect motives, cannot invalidate the nature either of beauty or of love.

On the contrary, it is as a gnostic that Ibn 'Arabī responded to the question of freedom; every creature does what it wills because every creature is basically what it wills to be: in other words, because a possibility is what it is and not something else. Freedom in the last analysis coincides with possibility, and this moreover is attested to by the Koranic story of the initial pact between human souls and God; destiny, consequently, is what the creature wills by his nature, and thus by his possibility. One may wonder which we should here admire more: the gnostic who penetrated the mystery or the philosopher who knew how to make it explicit.

But if man does what he is, or if he is what he does, why strive to become better and why pray to this end? Because there is the distinction between substance and accident: both demerits and merits come from either one or the other, without man being able to know from which they come, unless he is a "pneumatic" who is aware of his substantial reality, an ascending reality because of its conformity with the Spirit *(Pneuma)*, "Whoso knoweth his own soul, knoweth his Lord"; but even then, the effort belongs to man and the knowledge to God; that is to say, it suffices that we strive while being aware that God knows us. It suffices us to know that we are free in and through our movement towards God, our movement towards our "Self."

*

*   *

In a certain respect, the difference between philosophy, theology and gnosis is total; in another respect, it is relative. It is total when one understands by "philosophy," only rationalism; by "theology," only the explanation of religious teachings; and by "gnosis," only intuitive and intellective, and thus supra-rational, knowledge; but the difference is only relative when one understands by "philosophy" the fact of thinking, by "theology" the fact of speaking dogmatically of God and religious things, and by "gnosis" the fact of presenting pure metaphysics, for then the genres interpenetrate. It is impossible to deny that the most illustrious Sufis, while being "gnostics" by definition, were at the same time to some extent theologians and to some extent philosophers, or that the great theologians were both to some extent philosophers and to some extent gnostics, the last word having to be understood in its proper and not sectarian meaning.

If we wish to retain the limitative, or even pejorative, sense of the word philosopher, we could say that gnosis or pure metaphysics starts with certainty, whereas philosophy on the contrary starts from doubt and only serves to overcome it with the means that are at its disposal and which intend to be purely rational. But since neither the term "philosophy" in itself, nor the usage that has always been made of it, obliges us to accept only the restrictive sense of the word, we shall not censure too severely those who employ it in a wider sense than may seem opportune.[11]

Theory, by definition, is not an end in itself; it is only —and seeks only—to be a key for becoming conscious through the "heart." If there is attached to the notion of "philosophy" a suspicion of superficiality, insufficiency and pretension, it is precisely because all too often—and indeed always in the case of the moderns—it is presented as being sufficient unto itself. "This is only philosophy": we readily accept the use of this turn of phrase, but only on condition that one does not say that "Plato is only a philosopher," Plato who said that "beauty is the splendor of the true"; beauty that includes or demands all that we are or can be.

If Plato maintains that the *philosophos* should think independently of common opinions, he refers to intellection and not to logic alone; whereas a Descartes, who did everything to restrict and compromise the notion of philosophy, means it while starting from systematic doubt, so much so that for him philosophy is synonymous not only with rationalism, but also with skepticism. This is a first suicide of the intelligence, inaugurated moreover by Pyrrho and others, by way of a reaction against what was

11. Even Ananda Coomaraswamy does not hesitate to speak of "Hindu philosophy," which at least has the advantage of making clear the "literary genre," more especially as the reader is supposed to know what the Hindu spirit is in particular and what the traditional spirit is in general. In an analogous manner, when one speaks of the "Hindu religion," one knows perfectly well that it is not a case—and cannot be a case—of a Semitic and western religion, hence refractory to every differentiation of perspective; thus one speaks traditionally of the Roman, Greek and Egyptian "religions," and the Koran does not hesitate to say to the pagan Arabs: "To you your religion and to me mine," although the religion of the pagans had none of the characteristic features of Judeo-Christian monotheism.

believed to be metaphysical "dogmatism." The "Greek miracle" is in fact the substitution of the reason for the Intellect, of the fact for the Principle, of the phenomenon for the Idea, of the accident for the Substance, of the form for the Essence, of man for God; and this applies to art as well as to thought. The true Greek miracle, if miracle there be—and in this case it would be related to the "Hindu miracle"—is doctrinal metaphysics and methodic logic, providentially utilized by the monotheistic Semites.

*

* *

The notion of philosophy, with its suggestion of human fallibility, evokes *ipso facto* the problem of infallibility, and thereby the question of knowing whether man is condemned by his nature to be mistaken. We have seen in the course of this book that in fact the human mind, even when disciplined by a sacred tradition, remains exposed to many faults. That these should be possible does not mean that they are inevitable in principle; on the contrary they are due to causes that are not at all mysterious. Doctrinal infallibility pertains to the realm of orthodoxy and authority, the first element being objective and the second subjective, each having a bearing that is either formal or formless, extrinsic or intrinsic, traditional or universal, depending on the case. This being so, it is not even difficult to be infallible when one knows one's limits; it is enough not to speak of things of which one is ignorant, which presupposes that one knows that one is ignorant of them. This amounts to saying that infallibility is not only a matter of information and intellection, but that it also, and essentially, comprises a moral or a psychological condition, in the absence of which even men who are in principle infallible become accidentally fallible. Let us add that it is not blameworthy to offer a plausible hypothesis, on condition that is not be presented in the form of certitude *ex cathedra*.

At all events, no infallibility exists which *a priori* encompasses all possible contingent domains; omniscience is not a human possibility. No one can be infallible with regard to unknown, or insufficiently known, phenomena; one may have an intuition for pure principles without having one for a given phenomenal order, that is to say, without being able to apply the principles spontaneously in such and such a domain. The importance of this possible incapacity diminishes to the extent that the phenomenal domain envisaged is secondary and, on the contrary, that the principles infallibly enunciated are essential. One must forgive small errors on the part of one who offers great truths — and it is the latter that determine how small or how great the errors are — whereas it would obviously be perverse to forgive great errors when they are accompanied by many small truths.[12]

Infallibility, in a sense by definition, pertains in one degree or another to the Holy Spirit, in a way that may be extraordinary or ordinary, properly supernatural or quasi-natural; now the Holy Spirit, in the religious order, adapts itself to the nature of man in the sense that it limits itself to preventing the victory of intrinsic heresies, a victory which would falsify this "divine form" that is the religion; for the *upāya*, the "saving mirage," is willed by Heaven, not by men.[13]

12. There is certainly no reason to admire a science which counts insects and atoms but is ignorant of God; which makes an avowal of not knowing Him and yet claims omniscience by principle. It should be noted that the scientist, like every other rationalist, does not base himself on reason in itself; he calls "reason" his lack of imagination and knowledge, and his ignorances are for him the "data" of reason.

13. Always respectful of this form, the Holy Spirit will not teach a Moslem theologian the subtleties of trinitarian theology nor those of *Vedānta*; from another angle, it will not change a racial or ethnic mentality; neither that of the Romans in view of Catholicism, nor that of the Arabs in view of Islam. Humanity must not only have its history, but also its stories.

CHAPTER 6

The Quintessential Esoterism of Islam

The Islamic religion is divided into three constituent parts: *Imān*, Faith, which contains everything that one must believe; *Islām*, the Law, which contains everything that one must do; *Ihsān*,[1] operative virtue, which confers upon believing and doing the qualities that make them perfect, or in other words, which intensify or deepen both faith and works. *Ihsān*, in short, is the sincerity of the intelligence and the will: it is our total adhesion to the Truth and our total conformity to the Law, which means that we must, on the one hand, know the Truth entirely, not in part only, and on the other hand conform to it with our deepest being and not only with a partial and superficial will. Thus *Ihsān* converges upon esoterism—which is the science of the essential and the total—and is even identified with it; for to be sincere is to draw from the Truth the maximal consequences both from the point of view of the intelligence and from that of the will; in other words, it is to think and to will with the heart, and thus with our whole being, with all that we are.

Ihsān is right-believing and right-acting, and at the same time it is their quintessence: the quintessence of right-believing is metaphysical truth, the *Haqīqah*, and that of right-acting is the practice of invocation, the *Dhikr*. *Ihsān* comprises so to speak two modes, depending on its

---

1. Literally *Ihsān* means: "embellishment," "beautiful activity," "right-acting," "charitable activity"; and let us recall the relationship that exists in Arabic between the notions of beauty and virtue.

application: the speculative and the operative, namely intellectual discernment and unitive concentration; in Sufi language this is expressed exactly by the terms *Haqīqah*[2] and *Dhikr*, or by *Tawhīd*, "Unification," and *Ittihād*, "Union." For the Sufis, the "hypocrite" *(munāfiq)* is not only the one who gives himself airs of piety in order to impress people, but in a general way, one who is profane, who does not draw all the consequences that are implied in the Dogma and the Law, hence the man who is not sincere, since he is neither consequential nor whole; now Sufism *(tasawwuf)* is nothing other than sincerity *(sidq)* and the "sincere" *(siddīqūn)* are none other than the Sufis.

Ihsān, given that it is necessarily also an exoteric notion, may be interpreted at different levels and in different ways. Exoterically it is the faith of the fideists and the zeal of the ritualists; in which case it is intensity and not profundity and is thus something relatively quantitative or horizontal compared with wisdom. Esoterically, one can distinguish in *Ihsān* two accentuations, that of gnosis, which implies doctrinal intellectuality and that of love, which demands the totality of the volitive and emotive soul; the first mode operating with intellectual means— without for all that neglecting the supports that may be necessitated by human weakness—and the second, with moral and sentimental means. It is in nature of things that this love may exclude every element of intellection, and that it may readily if not always do so—precisely to the extent that it constitutes a way—whereas gnosis on the contrary always comprises an element of love, doubtless not violent love, but one akin to Beauty and Peace.

*

*   *

Ihsān comprises many ramifications, but it is quintessential esoterism that obviously constitutes it most direct-

2. It is to be noted that in the word *haqīqah*, as in its quasi-synonym *haqq*, the meanings "truth" and "reality" coincide.

ly. At first sight, the expression "quintessential esoterism" looks like a pleonasm; is not esoterism quintessential by definition? It is indeed so "by right," but not necessarily "in fact," as is amply proved by the unequal and often disconcerting phenomenon of average Sufism. The principal pitfall of this spirituality — let it be said once more — is the fact that in it metaphysics is treated according to the categories of an anthropomorphist and voluntaristic theology and of an individualistic piety above all obediential in character. Another pitfall, which goes hand in hand with the first, is the insistence on a certain hagiographic "mythology" and other preoccupations which enclose the intelligence and sensibility within the phenomenal order; finally, there is the abuse of scriptural interpretations and of metaphysico-mystical speculations, deriving from an ill-defined and ill-disciplined inspirationism, or from an esoterism which in fact is insufficiently conscious of its true nature.

An example of "moralizing metaphysics" is the confusion between a divine decree addressed to creatures endowed with free will, and the ontological possibility that determines the nature of a thing; and, resulting from this confusion, the affirmation that Satan, by disobeying God — or Pharaoh, by resisting Moses — obeyed God in that, by disobeying, they obeyed their archetype, and thus the existentiating divine "will," and that they have been — or will be — pardoned for this reason. Now the ideas of "divine will" and "obedience" are used here in an abusive manner, for in order that an ontological possibility be a "will" or an "order," it must emanate from the legislating Logos as such, and in this case it expressly concerns particular free and thereby responsible creatures; and in order that a submission, on the part of a thing or a being, be "obedience," it is necessary, in point of fact, that there be a discerning consciousness and freedom, and hence the possibility of not obeying. In the absence of this fundamental *distinguo*, there is merely doctrinal confusion and

131

misuse of language, and heresy from the legitimate point of view of the theologians.

The general impression given to us by Sufi literature must not make us forget that there were many Sufis who left no writings and who were strangers to the pitfalls that we have just described; their radiance has remained practically anonymous or has been merged with that of known personages. Indeed it may be that certain minds, instructed by the "vertical" way — and this refers to the mysterious filiation of Al-Khidr — and outside of the exigencies of a "horizontal" tradition made of underlying theology and dialectical habits, may have voluntarily abstained from formulating their thought in such an ambiance, without this having prevented the radiance proper to every spiritual presence.

To describe known or what one may call literary Sufism in all its *de facto* complexity and all its paradoxes, would require a whole book, whereas to give an account of the necessary and therefore concise character of Sufism, a few pages can suffice. "The Doctrine (and the Way) of Unity is unique" *(At-Tawhīdu wāhid)*: this classical formula expresses in concise manner the essentiality, primordiality and universality of Islamic esoterism as well as of esoterism as such; and we might even say that all wisdom or gnosis — all the *Advaita-Vedānta*, if one prefer — is for Islam, contained within the *Shahādah* alone, the two-fold Testimony of Faith.

Before going further, and in order to situate Islam within Monotheism, we wish to draw attention to the following: from the point of view of Islam, the religion of the primordial and the universal — analogically and principially speaking — Mosaism appears as a kind of "petrifaction," and Christianity, on the contrary, as a kind of "disequilibrium." In fact — leaving aside every question of exaggeration or stylization — Mosaism has the vocation of being the preserving ark of both the Abrahamic and the Sinaitic heritage, the "ghetto" of the One and Invisible

God, who speaks and acts, but who does so only for an Israel that is impenetrable and turned in on itself, and which puts all the emphasis on the Covenant and on obedience; whereas the sufficient reason for Christianity, at least as regards its specific mode, is to be the unprecedented and explosive exception that breaks the continuity of the horizontal and exteriorizing stream of the human by a vertical and interiorizing irruption of the Divine, the whole emphasis being put on the sacramental life and on penance. Islam, which professes to be Abrahamic, and therefore primordial, seeks to reconcile within itself all oppositions, just as the substance absorbs the accidents, without for all that abolishing their qualities; by referring to Abraham and thereby to Noah and Adam, Islam seeks again to bring out the value of the immense treasure of pure Monotheism, whence its accentuation on Unity and faith; it frees and reanimates this Monotheism, the Israelization and Christification of which had actualized particular potentialities, but dimmed its substantial light. All the unshakable certainty and all the propulsive power of Islam are explained by this, and cannot be explained otherwise.

*

*   *

The first Testimony of Faith *(Shahādah)* comprises two parts, each of which is composed of two words: *lā ilāha* and *illā 'Llāh*, "no divinity—except the (sole) Divinity." The first part, the "negation" *(nafy)*, corresponds to Universal Manifestation, which in regard to the Principle is illusory, whereas the second part, the "confirmation" *(ithbāt)*, corresponds to the Principle, which is Reality and which in relation to Manifestation is alone real.

And yet, Manifestation possesses a relative reality, lacking which it would be pure nothingness; complementarily, there must be within the principial order an element of relativity, lacking which this order could not be the cause of Manifestation, and therefore of what is relative by definition; this is what is expressed graphically by the Taoist symbol of the *Yin-Yang*, which is an image of compensatory reciprocity. That is to say, the Principle comprises at a lower degree than its Essence a prefiguration of Manifestation, which makes the latter possible; and Manifestation for its part comprises in its center a reflection of the Principle, lacking which it would be independent of the latter, which is inconceivable, relativity having no consistency of its own.

The prefiguration of Manifestation in the Principle— the principial Logos—is represented in the *Shahādah* by the word *illā* ("except" or "if not"), whereas the name *Allāh* expresses the Principle in itself; and the reflection of the Principle—the manifested Logos—is represented in its turn by the word *ilāha* ("divinity"), while the word *lā* ("there is no" or "no"), refers to Manifestation as such, which is illusory in relation to the Principle and consequently cannot be envisaged outside or separately from it.

This is the metaphysical and cosmological doctrine of the first Testimony, that of God *(lā ilāha illā 'Llāh)*. The doctrine of the second Testimony, that of the Prophet *(Muhammadun Rasūlu 'Llāh)*, refers to Unity, not exclusive this time, but inclusive; it enunciates, not distinction, but identity; not discernment, but union; not transcendence, but immanence; not the objective and macrocosmic discontinuity of the degrees of Reality, but the subjective and microcosmic continuity of the one Consciousness. The second Testimony is not static and separative like the first, but dynamic and unitive.

Strictly speaking, the second Testimony—according to the quintessential interpretation—envisages the Principle only in terms of three hypostatic aspects, namely: the manifested Principle *(Muhammad)*, the manifesting Principle *(Rasūl)* and the Principle in itself *(Allāh)*. The entire accent is put on the intermediate element, *Rasūl*, "Messenger"; it is this element, the Logos, that links the manifested Principle to the Principle in itself. The Logos is the "Spirit" *(Rūh)* of which it has been said that it is neither created nor uncreated or again, that it is manifested in relation to the Principle and non-manifested or principial in relation to Manifestation.

The word *Rasūl*, "Messenger," indicates a "descent" of God towards the world; it equally implies an "ascent" of man toward God. In the case of the Mohammedan phenomenon, the descent is that of the Koranic Revelation *(laylat al-qadr)*, and the ascent is that of the Prophet during the "Night Journey" *(laylat al-miʿrāj)*; in the human microcosm, the descent is inspiration, and the ascent is aspiration; the descent is divine grace, while the ascent is human effort, the content of which is the "remembrance of God" *(dhikru 'Llāh)*; whence the name *Dhikru 'Llāh* given to the Prophet. [3]

The three words *dhākir, dhikr, madhkūr*—a classical ternary in Sufism—correspond exactly to the ternary *Muhammad, Rasūl, Allāh: Muhammad* is the invoker, *Rasūl* the invocation, *Allāh* the invoked. In the invocation, the invoker and the invoked meet, just as *Muhammad* and *Allāh* meet in the *Rasūl*, or in the *Risālah*, the Message. [4]

The microcosmic aspect of the *Rasūl* explains the esoteric meaning of the "Blessing upon the Prophet" *(salāt ʿalā 'n-Nabī)*, which contains on the one hand the "Blessing" properly so called *(Salāt)* and on the other hand "Peace" *(Salām)*, the latter referring to the stabilizing, appeasing and "horizontal" graces, and the former to the transforming, vivifying and "vertical" graces. The "Prophet" is the immanent universal Intellect, and the purpose of the formula is to awaken within us the Heart-Intellect both in re-

3. Jacob's ladder is an image of the Logos, with the angels descending and ascending, God appearing at the top of the ladder, and Jacob remaining below.

4. Another ascending ternary is that of *makhāfah, mahabbah, maʿrifah*: fear, love, knowledge, modes which are both simultaneous and successive; we shall return to this later.

spect of receptivity and illumination; of the Peace that extinguishes and of Life that regenerates, by God and in God.

*

*   *

The first Testimony of Faith, which refers *a priori* to transcendence, comprises secondarily and necessarily a meaning according to immanence: in this case, the word *illā*, "except" or "if not," means that every positive quality, every perfection, every beauty, belongs to God or even, in a certain sense, "is" God, whence the Divine Name "the Outward" *(az-Zāhir)* which is complementarily opposed to "the Inward" *(al-Bātin)*.[5]

In an analogous but inverse manner, the second Testimony, which refers *a priori* to immanence, comprises secondarily and necessarily a meaning according to transcendence: in this case, the word *Rasūl*, "Messenger," means that Manifestation—*Muhammad*—is but the trace of the Principle, *Allāh*; that Manifestation is thus not the Principle.

These underlying meanings must accompany the main meanings by virtue of the principle of compensatory reciprocity to which we referred when speaking of the first Testimony, and in regard to which we made mention of the well-known symbol of *Yin-Yang*. For Manifestation is not the Principle, yet it is the Principle by participation, in virtue of its "non-inexistence"; and Manifestation—the word indicates this—is the Principle manifested, but without being able to be the Principle in itself. The unitive truth of the second Testimony cannot be absent from the first Testimony, any more than the separative truth of the first can be absent from the second.

5. This interpretation has given rise to the accusation of pantheism, wrongly of course, because God cannot be reduced to outwardness; in other words, because outwardness does not exclude inwardness, any more than immanence excludes transcendence.

And just as the first Testimony, which has above all a macrocosmic and objective meaning, also necessarily comprises a microcosmic and subjective meaning,[6] likewise the second Testimony, which has above all a microcosmic and subjective meaning also comprises, necessarily, a macrocosmic and objective meaning.

The two Testimonies culminate in the word *Allāh*, which being their essence contains them and thereby transcends them. In the name *Allāh*, the first syllable is short, contracted, absolute, while the second is long, expanded, infinite; it is thus that the Supreme Name contains these two mysteries, Absoluteness and Infinity, and thereby also the extrinsic effect of their complementarity, namely Manifestation, as is indicated by this *hadīth qudsī*: "I was a hidden treasure and I willed to be known, thus I created the world." Since absolute Reality intrinsically comprises Goodness, Beauty, Beatitude *(Rahmah)*, and since it is the Sovereign Good, it comprises *ipso facto* the tendency to communicate itself, thus to radiate; herein lies the aspect of Infinity of the Absolute; and it is this aspect that projects Possibility, Being, from which springs forth the world, things, creatures.

The Name *Muhammad* is that of the Logos, which is situated between the Principle and Manifestation, or between God and the world. Now the Logos, on the one hand is prefigured in the Principle, which is expressed by the word *illā* in the first *Shahādah*, and on the other hand projects itself into Manifestation, which is expressed by the word *ilāha* in the same formula. In the Name *Muhammad*, the whole accent and all the fulgurating power are situated at the center, between two short syllables, one

6. An initiatic or, one might say, "advaitic" sense: "There is no subject (no 'ego'), except the sole Subject (the 'Self')." It should be noted that Rāmana Maharshi, as well as Rāmakrishna, seem to have failed to recognize, in their teachings, the vital importance of the ritual and liturgical framework of the way, whereas neither the great Vedantists nor the Sufis ever lost sight of this.

initial and one final, without which this accentuation would not be possible; it is the sonorous image of the victorious Manifestation of the One.

*

*　*

According to the school of *Wujūdiyah*,[7] to say that "there is no divinity *(ilāha)* if not the (sole) Divinity *(Allāh)*" means that there is only God, that consequently everything is God, and that it is we creatures that see a multiple world where there is but one Reality; it remains to be seen why creatures see the One in multiple mode, and why God Himself, in so far as He creates, gives laws, and judges, sees the multiple and not the One. The correct answer is that multiplicity is objective as well as subjective—the cause of diversifying contingency being in each of the two poles of perception—and that multiplicity or diversity is in reality a subdivision, not of the Divine Principle of course, but of its manifesting projection, namely existential and universal Substance; diversity or plurality is therefore not opposed to Unity, it is within the latter and not alongside it. Multiplicity as such is the outward aspect of the world; however it is necessary to look at phenomena according to their inward reality, and thus as a diversified and diversifying projection of the One. The metacosmic cause of the phenomenon of multiplicity is All-Possibility, which coincides by definition with the Infinite, the latter being an intrinsic characteristic of the Absolute. The Divine Principle, being the Sovereign Good, tends by this very fact to radiate and thus to communicate itself; to project and to make explicit all the "possibilities of the Possible."

To say radiation is to say increasing distance, and thus progressive weakening or darkening, which explains

7. The ontological monism of Ibn 'Arabī. It should be noted that even in Islam this school does not have a monopoly on unitive metaphysics, in spite of the prestige of its founder.

the privative — and in the last analysis subversive — phenomenon of what we call evil; we call it such rightly, and in conformity with its nature, and not because of a particular, or even arbitrary, point of view. But evil, on pain of not being possible, must have a positive function in the economy of the universe, and this function is two-fold: there is firstly contrasting manifestation, in other words, the throwing into relief of the good by means of its opposite, for to distinguish a good from an evil is a way of understanding better the nature of the good;[8] then there is transitory collaboration which means that the role of evil is also to contribute to the realization of the good.[9] It is however absurd to assert that evil is a good because it is "willed by God" and because God can only will the good; evil always remains evil in respect of the privative or subversive character that defines it, but it is indirectly a good through the following factors: through existence, which detaches it so to speak from nothingness and makes it participate, together with everything that exists, in Divine Reality, the only one there is; through superimposed qualities or faculties, which as such always retain their positive character; and finally, as we have said, through its contrasting function with regard to the good and its indirect collaboration in the realization of the good.

To envisage evil in relation to cosmogonic Causality is

8. At first sight one might think that this throwing into relief is merely a secondary factor because it is circumstantial; but such is not the case since it is a question here of the quasi-principial opposition of phenomena — or of categories of phenomena — and not of accidental confrontations. Qualitative "constrasting" is indeed a cosmic principle and not a question of encounters or comparisons.

9. Evil in its aspect of suffering contributes to the unfolding of Mercy which, in order to be plenary, must be able to save in the fullest meaning of this word; that is to say that Divine Love in its dimension of unlimited compassion implies evil in its dimension of abysmal misery; to this the Psalms and the Book of Job bear witness, and to this the final and quasi-absolute solution is the Apocatastasis which integrates everything in the Sovereign Good.

at the same stroke and *a priori* to envisage it in relation to Universal Possibility: if manifesting radiation is necessarily prefigured in the Divine Being, the privative consequences of this Radiation must likewise be so, in a certain manner; not as such, of course, but as "punitive" functions — morally speaking — pertaining essentially to Power and Rigour, and consequently making manifest the "negation" *(nafy)* of the *Shahādah*, namely the exclusiveness of the Absolute. It is these functions that are expressed by the Divine Names of Wrath such as "He who contracts, tightens, tears *(Al-Qābid)*," "He who takes revenge *(Al-Muntaqim)*," "He who gives evil *(Ad-Dārr)*," and several others;[10] completely extrinsic functions, for: "Verily, my Mercy precedeth my Wrath *(Ghadab)*," as the inscription on the throne of *Allāh* declares; "precedes," and thus "takes precedence over," and in the last analysis "annuls." Moreover, the terrible divine functions, like the generous ones, are reflected in creatures, either positively by analogy, or negatively by opposition; for holy anger is something other than hatred, just as noble love is something other than blind passion.

We would add that the function of evil is to permit or to introduce the manifestation of Divine Anger, which means that the latter in a certain way creates evil with a view to its own ontologically necessary manifestation: if there is Universal Radiation, there is by virtue of the same necessity, both the phenomenon of evil and the manifestation of Rigor, then victory of the Good, thus the eminently compensatory manifestation of Clemency. We could also say, very elliptically, that evil is the "existence of the inexistant" or the "possibility of the impossible"; this

10. Vedantic doctrine discerns in the substantial or feminine pole *(Prakriti)* of Being three tendencies, one ascending and luminous *(Sattva)*, one expansive and fiery *(Rajas)* and one descending and obscure *(Tamas)*; this last does not in itself constitute evil, but it prefigures it indirectly and gives rise to it on certain levels or under certain conditions.

paradoxical possibility being required, as it were by the unlimitedness of All-Possibility, which cannot exclude even nothingness, however null in itself, yet "conceivable" both existentially as well as intellectually.

Whoever discerns and contemplates God, firstly in conceptual mode and then in the Heart, will finally see him also in creatures, in the manner permitted by their nature, and not otherwise. From this comes, on the one hand charity towards one's neighbor and on the other hand respect towards even inanimate objects, always to the extent required or permitted by their qualities and their defects, for it is not a question of deluding oneself but of understanding the real nature of creatures and things;[11] this means that one has to be just and, depending on the case, to be more charitable than just, and also that one must treat things in conformity with their nature and not with a profanating inadvertence. This is the most elementary manner of seeing God everywhere, and it is also to feel that we are everywhere seen by God; and since in charity there are no strict lines of demarcation, we would say that it is better to be a little too charitable than not charitable enough.[12]

*

* *

Each verse of the Koran, if it is not metaphysical or mystical in itself, comprises besides its immediate sense, a meaning that pertains to one or the other of these two domains; this certainly does not authorize one to put in the place of an underlying meaning an arbitrary and forced interpretation, for neither zeal nor ingenuity can replace

11. It is in this context as well that the love of beauty and the sense of the sacred are situated.

12. According to the Koran, God rewards merit much more than he punishes faults and He forgives the latter more readily on account of a little merit, than he lessens a reward on account of a little fault; always according to the measures of God, not according to ours.

141

the real intentions of the Text, whether these be direct or indirect, essential or secondary. "Lead us on the straight path": this verse refers first of all to dogmatic, ritual and moral rectitude; however, it cannot but refer also, and more especially, to the way of gnosis; on the contrary, when the Koran institutes some rule or other or when it relates some incident, no superior meaning imposes itself in a necessary way, which is not to say that this is excluded *a priori*, provided that the symbolism be plausible. It goes without saying that the exegetic science *('ilm al-uṣūl)* of the theologians, with its classification of explanatory categories, does not take account — and this is its right — of the liberties of esoterist readings.

A point that we must bring up here, even if only to mention it, is the discontinuous, allusive and elliptical character of the Koran: it is discontinuous like its mode of revelation or "descent" *(tanzīl)*, and allusive and therefore elliptical through its parabolism, which insinuates itself in secondary details, details that are all the more paradoxical in that their intention remains independent of the context. Moreover, it is a fact that the Arabs, and with them the Arabized, are fond of isolating and accentuating discontinuity, allusion, ellipsis, tautology and hyperbolism; all this seems to have its roots in certain characteristics of nomadic life, with its alternations, mysteries and nostalgias.[13]

Let us now consider the Koranic "signs" in them-

13. As regards allusive ellipsism, here are some examples: Solomon arrives with all his army in the "valley of the ants," and one of these says to the others: "O ants, go ye into your houses, so that Solomon and his troops do not crush you without knowing it." The meaning is, firstly, that the best of monarchs, to the very extent that he is powerful, cannot prevent injustices committed in his name, and secondly, that the small, when confronted with the great, must look to their own safety by remaining in a modest and discrete anonymity, and this not because of a voluntary ill will on the part of the great, but because of an inevitable situation; the subsequent prayer of Solomon expresses gratitude towards God, who gives all power, as well as the

selves. The following verses, and many others in addition, have an esoteric significance which if not always direct, is at least certain and therefore legitimate; or more precisely, each verse has several meanings of this kind, be it only because of the difference between the perspectives of love and gnosis, or between doctrine and method.

"God is the light of the heavens and of the earth (the Intellect that is both 'celestial' and 'terrestrial' = principial or manifested, macrocosmic or microcosmic, the transcendent or immanent Self)" (*Sura of Light*, 35); "And to God belong the East and the West. Wheresoe'er ye turn, there is the Face of God" (*Sura of the Cow*, 115); "He is the First and the Last and the Outward (the Apparent) and the Inward (the Hidden), and He knows infinitely all things" (*Sura of Iron*, 3); "He it is who hath sent down the

intention of being just, of "doing good." Then, Solomon, having inspected his troops, notices that the hoopoe, whose important function is to discover water holes, is absent, and he says: "Verily I shall punish it with a severe chastisement or I shall slay it, unless it give me a valid excuse"; the teaching which here slips into the general narrative is that it is a grave matter to fail, without a serious reason, in the duty of a function; the degrees of seriousness being expressed by the degrees of the punishment. Finally, the hoopoe having recounted that it had seen the queen of Sheba, the worshipper of the sun, Solomon says to it: "We wish to see if thou speakest the truth or if thou liest"; why this distrust? To emphasize that a leader must verify the reports of his subordinates, not because they are liars, but because they may be so; but the distrust of the king is also explained by the extraordinary nature of the account and it thereby comprises an indirect homage to the splendor of the kingdom of Sheba. These are so many psychological, social and political teachings inserted into the story of the meeting between Solomon and Queen Bilqîs (*Sura of the Ants*, 18, 21, 27); that these incidents can also have profound meanings we have no reason to doubt, without for all that wanting to abolish the distinction between interpretations which are necessary and those which are merely possible. Let us add, regarding the quotations given here, that it is completely in the style of Islam to mention — explicitly or implicitly — practical details which at first sight seem obvious, and thus to provide points of reference for the most diverse situations of individual and collective life; the Sunna is an abundant proof of this.

profound Peace (*Sakīnah* = Tranquillity through the Divine Presence) into the hearts of the believers (the heart being either the profound soul or the intellect), in order to add a faith unto their faith (an allusion to the illumination that superposes itself upon ordinary faith)" (*Sura of Victory*, 4); "Verily we belong to God and unto Him we shall return" (*Sura of the Cow*, 152); "And God calleth to the Abode of Peace and leadeth whom He will (whoever is qualified) on the straight (ascending) Path" (*Sura Yūnus*, 26); "Those who believe and those whose hearts find peace through the remembrance (mention = invocation) of God; is it not through the remembrance of God that hearts find peace?" (*Sura of the Cattle*, 91); "O men! Ye are the poor (*fuqarā'*, from *faqīr*) in relation to God and God is the Rich (*al-Ghanī* = the Independent), the universally Praised (every cosmic quality referring to Him and bearing witness to Him)" (*Sura of the Creator*, 15); "And the beyond (the principial night) is better for thee than the herebelow (the phenomenal world)" (*Sura of the Dawn*, 4); "And worship God until certainty (metaphysical certainty, gnosis) comes to thee" (*Sura of the Rock*, 99).

We have quoted these verses as examples, without undertaking to clarify the properly esoteric underlying meanings contained in their respective symbolisms. But it is not only the verses of the Koran that are important in Islam, there are also the sayings (*ahādīth*) of the Prophet, which obey the same laws and in which God sometimes speaks in the first person; a saying in this category to which we referred above, because of its doctrinal importance, is the following: "I was a hidden treasure and I willed to be known, and so I created the world." And a saying in which the Prophet speaks for himself, and which we also quoted, is the following: "Spiritual virtue (*ihsān* = right doing) is that thou shouldst worship God as if thou sawest Him, for, if thou seest Him not, He nevertheless seeth thee."

A key formula for Sufism is the famous *hadīth*, in

which God speaks through the mouth of the Messenger: "My slave ceaseth not to draw nigh unto Me by devotions freely accomplished,[14] until I love him; and when I love him, I am the hearing whereby he heareth and the sight whereby he seeth and the hand wherewith he smiteth and the foot whereon he walketh." It is thus that the Absolute Subject, the Self, penetrates into the contingent subject, the ego, and that the latter is reintegrated into the former; this is the principal theme of esoterism. The "devotions freely accomplished" culminate in the "remembrance of God" or are directly identified with it, all the more so since the profound reason for existence of every religious act is this remembrance, which in the last analysis is the reason for the existence of man.

But let us return to the Koran: the quasi-"eucharistic" element in Islam — in other words, the element of "heavenly nourishment" — is the psalmody of the Book; the Canonical Prayer is the obligatory minimum of this, but it contains, as if by compensation, a text that is considered to be the equivalent of the whole Koran, namely the *Fātihah*, the "Sura that opens." What is important in the rite of reading or reciting the Revealed Book is not only the literal understanding of the text, but also, and almost independently of this understanding, the assimilation of the "magic" of the Book, either by elocution, or by audition, with the intention of being penetrated by the Divine Word *(Kalāmu 'Llāh)* as such, and consequently forgetting the world and the ego.[15]

14. Exoterizing Sufism, which prolongs and intensifies the *Sharī'ah*, deduces from this passage the multiplication of pious practices, whereas the Sufism that is centered on gnosis deduces from it the frequency of the quintessential rite, the *Dhikr*, emphasizing its contemplative quality and not its character of meritorious act. Let us nevertheless remember that there is no strict line of demarcation between the two conceptions, although this line does exist by right and can always be affirmed.

15. It does happen that non-Arab Moslems, who to a large extent are ignorant of the language of the Koran, recite or read parts of

The sayings of Mohammed sometimes comprise judgements that seem excessive, which prompts us to give the following explanation. Ibn 'Arabī has been reproached for placing the Sages above the Prophets; wrongly, for he considered that all the Prophets were also Sages, but that the quality of wisdom took precedence over that of prophecy. The Sage indeed transmits truths as he perceives them whereas the Prophet as such transmits a Divine Will which he does not perceive spontaneously and which determines him in a moral and quasi-existential fashion; the Prophet is thus passive in his receptive function, whereas the Sage is active in his discernment, although in another respect the Truth is received passively, just as inversely and by way of compensation the Divine Will confers on the Prophet an active attitude. And here is the point we wish to make: when a Prophet proclaims a point of view whose limitations one can perceive without difficulty, starting from another religious system or from a perception of the nature of things, he does so because he incarnates a particular Divine Will. For example, there is a Divine Will which, in respect of one mentality, inspires the production of sacred images, just as there is another Divine Will which, in respect of another mentality, proscribes images; when the Arab Prophet, determined by this second Will, proscribes the plastic arts and anathematizes artists, he does so, not on the basis of a received opinion nor of a personal intellection, but under the effect of a Divine Will which takes possession of him and makes of him its instrument or spokesman.

All this is said to explain the "narrowness" of certain positions taken by the founders of religion. The Prophet

the Book in order to benefit from its *barakah*, a practice considered to be perfectly valid.

as a Sage has access to all truths, but there are some which
do not actualize themselves concretely in his mind or
which he puts in parentheses, unless an occasional cause
should make him change his attitude, and this depends on
Providence, not chance. The Prophet, by his nature, does
not belie as Sage what he has to personify as Prophet, except in a few exeptional cases which believers may understand or not understand, and of which they are not the
judges.

*
*   *

The two-fold Testimony is the first and the most important of the five "Pillars of the Religion" *(arkān ad-Dīn)*.
The others only have meaning in reference to it, and they
are the following: Canonical Prayer *(Salāt)*; the Fast of
Ramadan *(Siyām)*; Almsgiving *(Zakāt)*; Pilgrimage *(Hajj)*.
The esoterism of these practices resides not only in their
obvious initiatic symbolism, it resides also in the fact that
our practices are esoteric to the extent that we ourselves
are, firstly by our understanding of the Doctrine and then
by our assimilation of the Method;[16] these two elements
being contained, precisely, in the two-fold Testimony.
Prayer marks the submission of Manifestation to the
Principle; the Fast is detachment with regard to desires,
thus with regard to the ego; the Almsgiving is detachment
with regard to things, thus with regard to the world; the
Pilgrimage, finally, is the return to the Center, to the
Heart: to the Self. A sixth pillar is sometimes added, the
Holy War: this is the fight against the profane soul by
means of the spiritual weapon; it is therefore not the Holy
War that is outward and "lesser" *(asghar)*, but the Holy
War that is inward and "greater" *(akbar)*, according to a
hadīth. The Islamic initiation is in fact a pact with God

---

16. This essentially comprises the virtues, for there is no way
that is limited to an abstract and in a sense inhuman *yoga*; Sufism indeed is one of the most patent proofs of this.

147

with a view to this "greater" Holy War; the battle is fought by means of the *Dhikr* and on the basis of *Faqr*, inward Poverty; whence the name of *faqīr* given to the initiate.

Amongst the "Pillars of the Religion," that which the Prayer has in particular is that it has a precise form and comprises bodily positions which, being symbols, necessarily have meanings belonging to esoterism; but these meanings are simply explanatory, they do not enter consciously and operatively into the accomplishment of the rite, which only requires a sincere awareness of the formulas and a pious intention regarding the movements. The reason for the existence of the Canonical Prayer lies in the fact that man always remains an individual interlocutor before God and that he does not have to be anything else. When God wills that we speak to Him, He does not accept from us a metaphysical meditation. As regards the meaning of the movements of the Prayer, all that need be said here is that the vertical positions express our dignity as free and theomorphic vicar *(khalīfah)*, and that the prostrations on the contrary manifest our smallness as "servant" *('abd)* and as dependant and limited creature;[17] man must be aware of the two sides of his being, made as he is of clay and spirit.

*

* *

For obvious reasons, the Name *Allāh* is the quintessence of Prayer, as it is the quintessence of the Koran; containing in a certain manner the whole Koran, it thereby also contains the Canonical Prayer, which is the first sura of the Koran, "the opening" *(Al-Fātihah)*. In principle, the Supreme Name *(al-Ism al-A'zam)* even contains the whole religion, with all the practices that it demands,

17. The gestures of the ritual ablution *(wudū')*, without which man is not in a state of prayer, constitute various so to speak psychosomatic purifications. Man sins with the members of his body, but the root of sin is in the soul.

and it could consequently replace them;[18] but in fact, these practices contribute to the equilibrium of the soul and of society, or rather they condition them.

In several passages, the Koran enjoins the faithful to remember God, and thus to invoke Him, and frequently repeat His Name. Likewise, the Prophet said: "It behoves you to remember your Lord (to invoke Him)." He also said: "There is a means of polishing every thing, and of removing rust; what polishes the heart is the invocation of *Allāh*; and there is no act which removes God's punishment as much as does this invocation." The Companions (of the Prophet) said: "Is the fight against infidels equal to that?" He replied: "No, not even if one fights until one's sword is broken." And he said further, on another occasion: "Should I not teach you an action that is better for you than fighting against infidels?" His Companions said: "Yes, teach us." The Prophet said: "This action is the invocation of *Allāh*."

18. "Remembrance *(dhikr)* is the most important rule of the religion . . . the Law was not imposed upon us, neither were the rites of worship ordained but for the sake of establishing the remembrance of God *(dhikru 'Llāh)*. The Prophet said: The circumambulation *(tawāf)* around the Holy House, the passage to and fro between (the hills of) Safā and Marwah and the throwing of the pebbles (on three pillars symbolizing the devil), were only ordained with a view to the Remembrance of God. — And God Himself has said (in the Koran): Remember God at the Holy Monument. — Thus we know that the rite that consists in stopping there was ordained for remembrance and not specially for the sake of the monument itself, just as the halt at Muna was ordained for remembrance and not because of the valley . . . Furthermore He (God) has said on the subject of the ritual prayer: Perform the prayer in remembrance of Me. — In a word, our performance of the rites is considered ardent or lukewarm according to the degree of our remembrance of God while performing them. Thus when the Prophet was asked which spiritual strivers would receive the greatest reward, he replied: those who have remembered God most. — And when the prayer and the almsgiving and the pilgrimage and the charitable donations were mentioned, he said of each: The richest in remembrance of God is the richest in reward." (The Shaykh Ahmad Al-'Alawī in his treatise *Al-Qawl al-Ma'rūf*).

The *Dhikr*, which implies spiritual combat since the soul tends naturally towards the world and the passions, coincides with the *Jihād*, the Holy War; the Islamic initiation — as we said above — is a pact with a view to this War; a pact with the Prophet and with God. The Prophet, on returning from a battle declared: "We have returned from the lesser Holy War (performed with the sword) to the greater Holy War (performed with invocation)."

The *Dhikr* contains the whole Law *(Sharī'ah)* and it is the reason for the existence of the whole Law;[19] this is declared by the Koranic verse: "Verily prayer (the exoteric practice) prevents man from committing what is shameful (sullying) and blameworthy; and verily the remembrance (invocation) of God (the esoteric practice) is greater." *(Sura of the Spider,* 45).[20] The formula "the remembrance of God is greater" or "the greatest thing" *(wa la-dhikru 'Llāhi akbar)* evokes and paraphrases the following words from the Canonical Prayer: "God is greater" or "the greatest" *(Allāhu akbar)* and this indicates a mysterious connection between God and His Name; it also indicates a certain relativity — from the point of view of gnosis — of the outward rites, which are nevertheless indispensable in principle and in the majority of cases. In this connection we could also quote the following *hadīth*: one of the Companions said to the Prophet: "O Messenger of God, the prescriptions of Islam are too numerous for me; tell me something that I can hold fast to." The Prophet replied: "Let thy tongue always be supple (in movement) with the mention (the remembrance) of God." This *hadīth*, like the verse we have just quoted, expresses by allusion *(ishārah)*

---

19. This is the point of view of all invocatory disciplines, such as the Hindu *japa-yoga* or the Amidist *nembutsu (buddhānusmriti)*. This *yoga* is found in *jnāna* as well as in *bhakti*: "Repeat the Sacred Name of the Divinity," said Shankarāchārya in one of his hymns.

20. "God and His Name are identical," as Rāmākrishna said; and he certainly was not the first to say so.

the principle of the inherence of the whole *Sharī'ah* in the *Dhikr* alone.

"Verily ye have in the Messenger of God a fair example for whosoever hopeth in God and in the Last Day and remembereth God much." (*Sura of the Confederates*, 21). "Whosoever hopeth in God": this is he who accepts the Testimony, the *Shahādah*, not merely with his mind, but also with his heart; this is expressed by the word "hopeth." Now faith in God implies by way of consequence faith in our final ends; and to act in consequence is quintessentially to "remember God"; it is to fix the spirit on the Real instead of dissipating it in the illusory; and it is to find peace in this fixation, according to the verse quoted above: "Is it not in the remembrance of God that hearts find peace?"

"God makes firm those who believe by the firm Word, in the life of this world and in the beyond." (*Sura Ibrāhīm*, 27). The "firm Word" *(al-qawl ath-thābit)* is either the *Shahādah*, the Testimony, or the *Ism*, the Name, the nature of the *Shahādah* being *a priori* intellectual or doctrinal, and that of the *Ism* being existential or alchemical; but not in an exclusive manner, for each of the two Divine Words participates in the other, the Testimony being in its way a Divine Name and the Name being implicitly a doctrinal Testimony. By these two Words, man becomes rooted in the Immutable, in this world as in the next. The "firmness" of the Divine Word refers quintessentially to the Absolute, which in Islamic language is the One; also, the affirmative part of the *Shahādah*—the words *illā 'Llāh*—is called a "firming" *(ithbāt)*, which indicates reintegration into immutable Unity.

The whole doctrine of the *Dhikr* emerges from these words: "And remember Me *(Allāh)*, I shall remember you *(Fadhkurūnī adhkurkum)*" (*Sura of the Cow*, 152). This is the doctrine of mystical reciprocity, as it appears in the following saying of the early Church: "God became man so that man become God"; the Essence became form so that form become Essence. This presupposes within the Essence a formal potentiality, and within form a mysterious immanence of the essential Reality; the Essence unites because it is one.

*

* *

Every way comprises successive stages which can at the same time be simultaneous modes; these are the "stations" (*maqāmāt*, singular: *maqām*), of Sufism. The fundamental stations are three in number: "Fear" *(Makhāfah)*, "Love" *(Mahabbah)* and "Knowledge" *(Ma'rifah)*; the number — in principle indeterminate — of the other stations is obtained by the subdivision of the three fundamental stations, either through the ternary being reflected in each of them, or by each one being polarized into two complementary stations, each of which may in its turn comprise various aspects, and so on. Moreover the "stations" are also manifested as passing "states" *(ahwāl,* singular: *hāl)* which are anticipations of the former or cause a station already acquired to participate in another station still unexplored.

That each of the three fundamental modes of perfection or of the way is repeated or reflected in the two other modes, appears obvious and easy to imagine; we shall therefore not seek here to describe these reciprocal reverberations. However, we must give an account of a subdivision which is not self-explanatory, and which results from the bipolarization of each mode by reason of the universal law of complementarity; for example, this is expressed in a fundamental manner by the Divine Names "the Immutable" *(Al-Qayyūm)* and "the Living" *(Al-Hayy)*. Thus, we may distinguish within *Makhāfah* a static pole, abstention or Renunciation *(Zuhd)*, and a dynamic pole, Accomplishment or Effort *(Jahd)*; the first pole realizing "Poverty" *(Faqr)*, without which there is no valid work, and the second giving rise to "remembrance" *(Dhikr)*, which is work in the highest sense of the word and which eminently contains all works; not from the point of view of worldly necessities or opportunities, but from that of the fundamental demands of God.

In *Mahabbah* likewise, there are grounds for distinguishing between a static or passive pole and a dynamic or active pole: the first is Contentment *(Ridā)* or Gratitude *(Shukr)*, and the second, Hope *(Rajā')* or Confidence *(Tawakkul)*. The latter, moreover, implies Generosity *(Karam)*, just as Contentment for its part implies or requires Patience *(Sabr)*; these virtues are necessarily relative, and thus conditional, except towards God.[21]

Ma'rifah, for its part, comprises an objective pole which refers to transcendence and a subjective pole which refers to immanence: on the one hand there is "Truth" *(Haqq)* or Discernment of the One *(Tawhīd)*, and on the other hand, the "Heart" *(Qalb)* or Union with the One *(Ittihād)*.

The three formulas of the Sufi rosary retrace the three fundamental degrees or planes: the "Asking of forgiveness" *(Istighfār)* correspnds to "Fear"; the "Blessing of the Prophet" *(Salāt 'alā 'n-Nabī)*, to "Love"; the "Testimony of Faith" *(Shahādah)*, to "Knowledge." The higher planes always include the lower planes, while the latter prefigure or anticipate the former, be it only by opening onto them, for Reality is one, in the soul as in the Universe. Moreover, Action rejoins Love to the extent that it is disinterested; and it rejoins Knowledge to the extent that it is accompanied by an awareness that God is the true Agent; and the same applies to Abstention, the *vacare Deo*, which also can only have its source in God, in the sense that mystical emptiness prolongs the principial Void.

---

21. We give here only the "archetypes" or "keys" of the virtues — or "stations" — which sum up their multiple derivations. The *Risālah* of Qushairī or the *Mahāsin al-Majālis* of Ibn Al-'Arīf, and other treatises of this kind, contain enumerations and analyses of these subdivisions, which have been studied by various Arabists.

In fact, classical Sufism has a tendency to seek to obtain cognitive results by volitive means, rather than seeking to obtain volitive results by cognitive means, or by what are intellectual evidences;[22] the two attitudes must in reality be combined, especially since, in Islam, the supreme and decisive merit is acceptance of a truth and not moral attitude. Unquestionably, profound virtues predispose to Knowledge and can, in cases of heroicalness, even bring about its blossoming, but it is no less true, to say the least, that when the Truth is well assimilated it produces the virtues, to the very proportion of this assimilation or, what amounts to the same, of this qualification.

*

*   *

The Koran repeatedly quotes the names of earlier Prophets and relates their stories; this must have a meaning for our spiritual life, as the Koran moreover makes clear. It can happen indeed, that a Sufi is attached, within the frameword of the Mohammedan Way itself — which is his by definition — to some pre-Islamic Prophet; in other words, the Sufi places himself under the symbol, influence, affective direction, of a Prophet who personifies a congenial vocation. Islam sees in Christ — Sayyidnā 'Isā — the personification of renunciation, interiorization, contemplative and solitary sanctity, and Union; and more than one Sufi claimed this spiritual filiation.

The series of great Semitic Prophets comprises only one woman, Sayyidatnā Maryam; her prophetic — but not law-giving — dignity is made clear from the way the Koran presents her, and also from the fact that she is mentioned, in the *Sura of the Prophets*, together with other Messengers. Maryam incarnates inviolable purity to which is joined divine fecundation;[23] she also personifies

22. As was understood by the best of the Greeks, the word "philosophy" implied for them virtue through wisdom.

23. "And Maryam, daughter of 'Imrān, who kept her virginity

spiritual retreat and abundance of graces,[24] and in an altogether general manner and *a priori*, celestial Femininity, Purity, Beauty, Mercy. The Message of the Blessed Virgin was Jesus, not Jesus as founder of a religion, but the Child Jesus;[25] not such and such a *Rasūl*, but the *Rasūl* as such, who contains all the prophetic forms possible in their universal and primordial indifferentiation. Thus it is that the Virgin is considered, by certain Sufis as well as by Christian authors, as Wisdom-Mother, or as Mother of Prophecy and of all the Prophets; hence Islam calls her *Siddīqah*, the "Sincere"—sincerity being none other than total conformity to the Truth—which is indicated by the identification of Mary with Wisdom or with Sanctity in itself.

*

* *

The Sufi willingly calls himself, "son of the Moment" *(ibn al-Waqt)*; that is to say, he is situated in God's Present without caring for yesterday or tomorrow, and this Present is none other than a reflection of Unity; the One projected into time becomes the "Now" of God which coincides with Eternity. The Sufi cannot call himself the "son

---

intact; and We *(Allāh)* breathed into her of Our Spirit *(Rūh)*" (*Sura of the Banning*, 12).

24. According to the Koran, Mary spent her early youth in the "prayer-niche" *(mihrāb)* of the Temple; she was nourished there by angels. When Zacharias asked her whence came this food, the Virgin replied: "It comes from God, verily God provides sustenance for whom He will beyond all reckoning." (*Sura of the Family of 'Imrān*, 37). The image of the "prayer niche"—or of the spiritual retreat *(khalwah)*—is found in the following verse: "And mention (O Prophet), in the Book, Maryam: when she withdrew from her family (from the world) to a place facing the East (facing the Light); and she placed a veil between her and her people . . . " (*Sura Maryam*, 16 and 17).

25. "And We *(Allāh)* have made of the Son of Maryam and his Mother a sign *(āyah)*." (*Sura of the Believers*, 50). It will be noted that the "sign" is not Jesus alone, but he and his Mother.

of the One," for this expression would evoke Christian terminology, which Islam must exclude because of its perspective; but he could call himself "son of the Center" — according to spatial symbolism this time — and he does so indirectly by his insistence on the mysteries of the Heart.

The whole of Sufism, it seems to us, is summed up in these four words: *Haqq*, *Qalb*, *Dhikr*, *Faqr*: "Truth," "Heart," "Remembrance," "Poverty." *Haqq* coincides with the *Shahādah*, the two-fold Testimony: the metaphysical, cosmological, mystical and eschatological Truth. *Qalb* means that this Truth must be accepted, not by the mind alone, but with the Heart, thus with all that we are. *Dhikr*, as we know, is the permanent actualization, by means of the sacramental word, of this Faith or this Gnosis; while *Faqr* is simplicity and purity of soul, which make possible this actualization by conferring on it the sincerity without which no act is valid.[26]

The four most important formulas in Islam, which correspond in a certain sense to the four rivers of Paradise gushing forth from beneath the Throne of *Allāh* — the earthly reflection of this throne being the Kaaba — are the first and second *Shahādahs*, then the Consecration and the Praise: the *Basmalah* and the *Hamdalah*. The first *Shahādah*: "There is no divinity except the (sole) Divinity"; the second *Shahādah*: "Mohammed is the Messenger of God (of the sole Divinity)"; the *Basmalah*: "In the Name of God, the Clement, the Merciful";[27] the *Hamdalah*: "Praise be to God, the Lord of the worlds."

26. "Blessed are the pure in heart, for they shall see God." (*Matthew*, V, 8).

27. God is clement or benevolent in Himself, in the sense that Goodness, Beauty and Love are comprised in His very Essence *(Dhāt)* and that He therefore manifests them necessarily in and through the world; this is expressed by the Name *Rahmān*, which is almost synonymous with the Name *Allāh*. And God is in addition good towards the world in the sense that He manifests His goodness towards creatures by according them subsistence and all possible gifts, including eminently salvation; it is this that is expressed by the Name *Rahīm*.

CHAPTER 7

Hypostatic Dimensions of Unity

Let us now return by way of conclusion, since our intentions converge on the quintessence, to the metaphysical synthesis that we outlined when we referred to the esoteric symbolism of the *Shahādah*. The fundamental idea of
Islam, that of Divine Unity, necessarily implies the idea
of diversity, or the idea of the relationships between the
One and that which seems to invalidate or contradict it;
here we shall deal with this problem in a necessarily concise manner and, of course, without losing sight of the fact
that a doctrinal schema can offer no more than landmarks, if only for the simple reason that an expression is
of necessity something other than the reality expressed.
Identity between the schema and the reality is moreover
as unnecessary as it is impossible, precisely because the
schema is capable of providing perfectly sufficient landmarks; otherwise there would be no adequate and effective symbolism, nor consequently any doctrine.

The whole problem of creation, or of universal manifestation, has its root in the very nature of the Divine
Principle. The Absolutely Real projects the world because
its infinite nature requires that it also be known starting
from relativity and within it; to say that God "created"
and not that He "creates," is a way of expressing the con-
tengency or the relativity of the world and in a certain
sense it is to cut off the latter from its transcendent Cause.
God "wills to be seen" not only "starting" from the world,
but also "in" the world and even "as" world: either directly

157

in qualities, or indirectly and by contrast in their absence; and He wills to be seen, not only by man, but also by the lower creatures, who contemplate Him in a certain fashion by their specific form itself, or at least by whatever is positive in their form or in their state, as the case may be.

Absolute, Infinite, Perfection: these, we might say, are the primary definitions of the divine nature. Geometrically speaking, the Absolute is like the point, which excludes everything that is not itself; the Infinite is like the cross, or the star, or the spiral, which prolong the point and in a sense make it inclusive; and Perfection is like the circle, or the system of concentric circles, which reflects or transposes the point into extension. The Absolute is Ultimate Reality in itself; the Infinite is its Possibility, and thus also its Omnipotence; Perfection is Possibility insofar as the latter realizes a given potentiality of the Absolutely Real, or insofar as it realizes all Potentialities. Creation, or manifestation, is an effect of the Divine Nature: God cannot prevent Himself from radiating, and thus manifesting Himself or creating, because He cannot prevent Himself from being infinite.

The Divine Perfection is the sum or quintessence of all possible perfections, finally, we know them by experience; these perfections are manifested thanks to the Infinite, which offers them existential space, or substance if one prefers, and which actualizes and projects them; and it is thanks to the Absolute that things exist, or that they are not "inexistent." The Absolute, imperceptible in itself, makes itself visible by the existence and by the logic of things; in an analogous manner, the Infinite reveals itself by their inexhaustible diversity; likewise again, Perfection manifests itself by their qualities, and in so doing it communicates both the rigor of the Absolute and the radiation of the Infinite, for things have their musicality as well as their geometry. In other words: when everyday natural experience is combined with metaphysical intuition or with faith — and the latter always actualizes the former to a certain degree — the recognition of the positive qualities in things and beings obliges us to accept their archetypes or their essences in the divine Order; likewise, the inconceivability of limits in space-time obliges us to accept the Infinite in itself; likewise again, the fact that the least existence is absolute in relation to its absence — or the fact that physical, mathematical and logical laws are ineluctable — bears witness, in the last analysis, to the Absolute and leaves us with no other choice than to accept it.[1]

*

* *

The ternary "Absolute-Infinite-Perfection" is reflected in the progression of numbers: the number one corresponds to the Absolute, the progression to the Infinite, and the particular character — the form of each number — to Perfection.[2] The progression of numbers is not properly speaking comparable to an indefinite series of points of which one is necessarily the first, as if there could be a progression with a beginning, but not an end, in reality, we must compare the number one to the central point and the progression to an indefinite series of concentric circles; the center has the value of an absolute by definition, thus it is not a beginning properly speaking; it is as it were outside number, but the latter is inconceivable without the former. The same is true of the unlimited diversity of forms: the central form is circular or spherical, and there is no common measure between it and the square or the cube; roundness has something absolute about it in relation to all other possible forms. Another example of existential progression is provided by matter, in which the

1. No doubt this way of thinking is meaningless to rationalists, but what matters, is that they can in no wise prove the opposite, either from the objective point of view of the Real, or from the subjective point of view of knowledge.
2. As is shown by geometrical figures insofar as they express numbers, which in this respect are qualities and not quantities.

four sensible elements and all chemical aggregates and substances emerge from ether which, being simple — and inherent in every sensible substance — is the center of this unfolding. Here too, the central element cannot be merely a so to speak quantitative beginning; quite to the contrary, it is quasi-transcendent in relation to its modalities or projections. Since the modalities are "infinite" in number, unity or the center must have an "absolute" character.

The ternary "Absolute-Infinite-Perfection" finds its most direct expression, in Islamic language, in the terms *Jalāl, Jamāl* and *Kamāl*: "Majesty," "Beauty" and "Perfection." Traditionally, Rigor or Justice is attributed to Majesty, and Gentleness or Mercy to Beauty; now Beauty like Mercy pertains to the Infinite; and Majesty, like Justice, to the Absolute.

*
*   *

There is a profound significance in the fact, at first sight paradoxical, that Islam, jealous as it is of the unity of God and so scrupulous in its fundamental formulations, puts at the head of each sura the in a sense trinitarian formula "In the Name of God, the Clement, the Merciful," and that it employs this formula on every occasion as a consecratory blessing. We think we have already provided the key to the enigma; namely, that when we speak of the Absolute, we speak by the same token of the Infinite and the Perfect.[3] *Rahmah* — a term that is most of-

---

3. In Christianity, the element "Absolute" is represented either analogically or directly by the "Father"; the element "Infinite" or "Radiation" being the Holy Spirit, and the element "Perfection," the "Son" or the Word, which is the "Wisdom of the Father." In Buddhism, it is the Buddha who represents Perfection while, in a manner that is at first sight paradoxical, Radiation is presented in the form of the *Boddhisattva*, who in fact carries the message of *Nirvana* — of the Absolute — to the extremity of the *Samsāra*.

ten translated as "Clemency"—implies more profoundly, as does the Sanskrit term *Ananda*, all the aspects of Harmony:[4] Goodness, Beauty and Beatitude; and *Rahmah* is integrated into the Divine Essence itself, inasmuch as it is fundamentally none other than the radiating Infinitude of the Principle; an identity that the Koran expresses by saying: "Call upon *Allāh* or call upon *Ar-Rahmān*, to Him belong the most beautiful Names . . . ".[5]

For one cannot appeal to the One without Mercy responding.

*

* *

God is manifested in the world, as we have said, by the miracle of existence, the gulf between the least grain of dust and nothingness being absolute; He manifests His Infinity *a priori* by the cosmic container space-time, which has no imaginable limits, any more than do the multiplicity and diversity of its contents; and He manifests His Perfection by the qualities of things and beings, which bear witness to their divine archetypes and thereby to the Divine Perfection.

This triple manifestation constitutes the Divine "Outwardness," which is expressed by the Name "the Outward" *(Az-Zāhir)*. According to the Sufis, the *Shahādah*

4. *Sat* referring to the Absolute, and *Chit* to the Consciousness that *Atmā* has of its inexhaustible Perfection, hence of its Qualities.

5. A remark: the Trinity which the Koran attributes to Christianity—namely "God, Jesus, Mary"—is justified in the sense that the Holy Virgin is by her nature, and not by adoption, the human receptacle of the Holy Spirit (whence *gratia plena* and *Dominus tecum*); as "Immaculate Conception," she is *a priori* the vehicle of the Spirit and thereby personifies it. It follows that an invocation of Mary, such as the *Ave*, is practically, implicitly and quintessentially an invocation of the Holy Spirit, which in Islam pertains to the hypostatic mystery of *Rahmānīyah*, Divine "Generosity" which is Life, Radiation, Light; the Virgin, like the Spirit, is the "womb" *(rahim)*, both inviolable and generous, of all graces.

comprises two meanings, depending on whether one has in mind transcendence or immanence: firstly, the truth that God alone is real, as opposed to the world which, being contingent, is illusory; then the truth that no existence can be situated outside God: that all that exists "is not other than He" *(lā ghayruhu)*, failing which, precisely the world would not exist. The first meaning corresponds to the mystery of the "Inward" *(Al-Bātin)*, and the second, to that of "the Outward."

It is not true that we cannot know what God is and that we can only know what He is not; but it is true that we cannot imagine God, any more than we can hear light or see thunder. On the one hand, space together with time, then the existence of things, and then their qualities, "prove" God; on the other hand, they "are" God, but seen through the veil of "Outwardness" or of "Distance" *(bu'd)*, and thus of contingency. This veil produces by definition the privative or subversive phenomenon of evil, which is the ransom of projection outside the Principle; a projection which is nevertheless necessary and finally benefic since "I was a hidden treasure and I willed to be known": for Universal Radiation is the very consequence of the "Sovereign Good."

The Absolute, or the Essence, intrinsically comprises Infinitude; it is as the Infinite that it radiates. Divine Radiation projects the Essence into the "void," but without there being any "going out" whatsoever, for the Principle is immutable and indivisible, nothing can be taken away from it; by this projection on the surface of a nothingness that in itself is inexistent, the Essence is reflected in the mode of "forms" or "accidents." But the "life" of the Infinite is not only centrifugal, it is also centripetal; it is alternately or simultaneously — depending on the relationships envisaged — Radiation and Reintegration; the latter is the apocatastatic "return" of forms and accidents into the Essence, without nevertheless there being anything added to the latter, for it is absolute Plenitude. Moreover, and

162

even above all, Infinitude—like Perfection—is an intrinsic characteristic of the Absolute: it is as it were its inward life, or its love which by overflowing, so to speak prolongs itself and creates the world.

*

* *

Certainty and serenity: the fundamental intention of Islam is contained in these two words. For everything begins with certainty: certainty of the Absolute *(Wujūd al-mutlaq)*, of "necessary" Being, which projects and determines "possible" existences. Certainty of that which, being necessary, cannot not be, whereas contingencies may either be or not be; and serenity by finding one's roots in that which is.

Certainty is saving to the extent that it is objectively lofty and subjectively sincere; that is to say: to the extent that its object is the Absolute, not mere contingency, and that its subject is the heart, not thought alone. This certainty is the very essence of man, it includes the whole of his being and the whole of his activity; man was made and created for it, and he is man through it.

Certainty produces serenity; serenity penetrates the soul, it is the radiation of liberating certainty. Serenity is to certainty what the Infinite is to the Absolute, or what Possibility is to Reality, or Totality to Unity. Certainty and serenity are prolonged in faith.

Certainty, serenity and faith: by and through this necessary and free Being which alone gives a meaning to all that is, in the world and in man, and which is Light, Peace and Life.